MACHINES OF THE MIND

Sculpture by Lawrence Fane

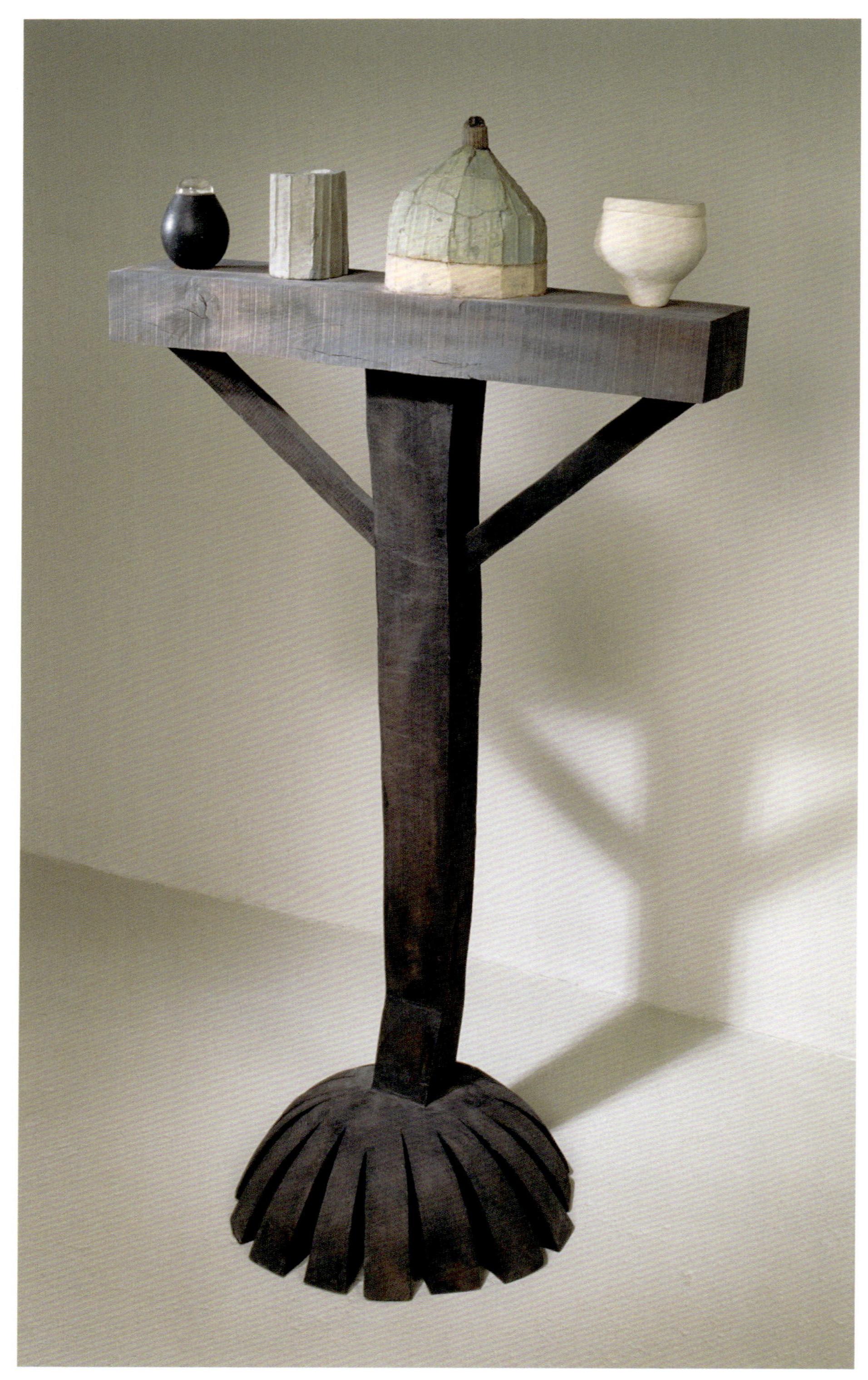

MACHINES OF THE MIND

Sculpture by Lawrence Fane

MARSH ART GALLERY

UNIVERSITY OF RICHMOND MUSEUMS

April 3 to June 29, 2002

MUSCARELLE MUSEUM OF ART

THE COLLEGE OF WILLIAM AND MARY

March 30 to May 12, 2002

Published on the occasion of the exhibition
Machines of the Mind: Sculpture by Lawrence Fane

Marsh Art Gallery, University of Richmond Museums
April 3 to June 29, 2002

Muscarelle Museum of Art, The College of William and Mary
March 30 to May 12, 2002

Organized by the Marsh Art Gallery, University of Richmond Museums,
in collaboration with the Muscarelle Museum of Art, The College of William and Mary,
Williamsburg, Virginia, the exhibition occurs simultaneously at both museums.
The exhibition at the Marsh Art Gallery, University Museums, is part of a yearlong
Festival of American Arts and is made possible in part with a grant from
the University of Richmond Cultural Affairs Committee.

The exhibition catalogue is made possible in part with the generous support of
The Cowles Charitable Trust and The Richard Florsheim Art Fund.

Published by University of Richmond Museums,
Richmond, Virginia 23173 (804) 289-8276

Printed by Worth Higgins & Associates Inc., Richmond, Virginia

Cover: *Conduit* (detail)
2000, concrete and wood, stains, 62 x 47 x 86 inches
Collection of the artist
(cat. no. 26; full illustration, p. 6)

Frontispiece: *Colmar*
2000, wood, cement, plastic, stains, 59 x 30 x 18 inches
Collection of the artist
(cat. no. 27)

Library of Congress Control Number: 2002103706
ISBN 0-9713753-2-1

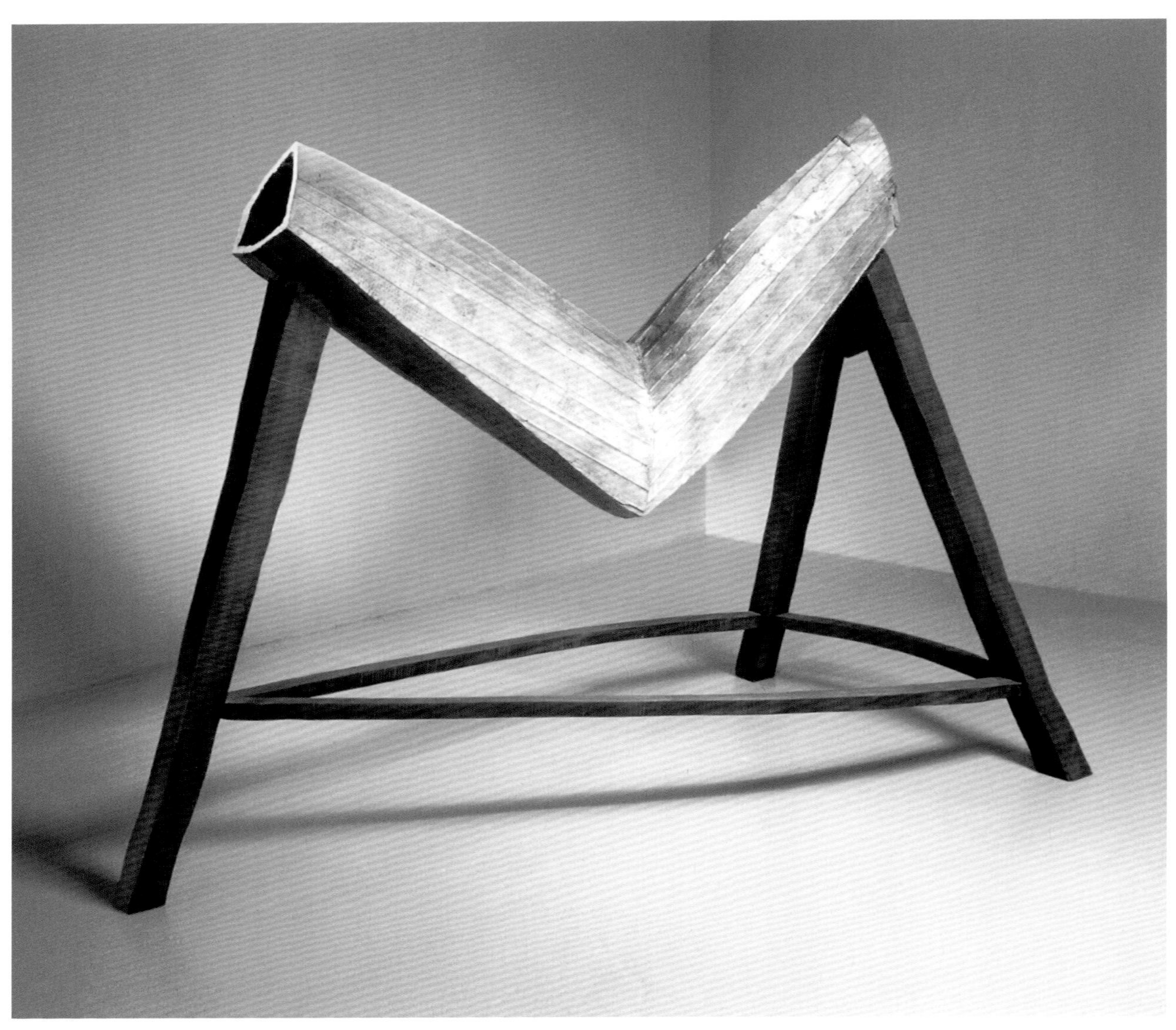

Conduit

2000

concrete and wood, stains, 62 x 47 x 86 inches

Collection of the artist

(cat. no. 26)

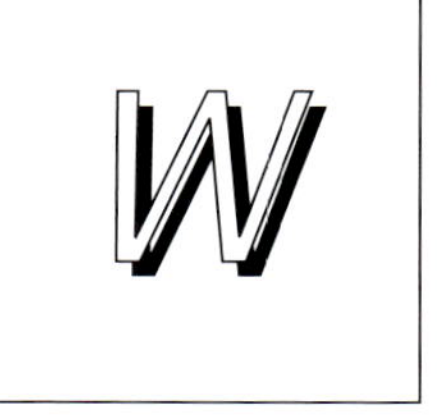

W E ARE PLEASED TO PRESENT this exhibition of the sculptures of Lawrence Fane. Occurring at two museums at the same time, the Muscarelle Museum of Art and the Marsh Art Gallery, we are able to present a larger selection of the artist's recent sculptures and, thus, give a better experience of Fane's "machines of the mind." Aptly titled, the exhibition presents the remarkable works he has created, primarily from the last twelve years, that appear to be archaic, machine-like artifacts made from carved wood, steel, and cast concrete. Suggesting objects of uncertain function and ritual, Fane's sculptures evoke humanized machines that seem to merge the beauty and power of the mechanical with that of natural forms.

The successful realization of the exhibition is due to the invaluable contributions of numerous people. First and foremost, our deepest thanks go to the artist, Lawrence Fane, who has been so wonderfully helpful and gracious throughout the entire organization of the exhibition and the catalogue.

We are indebted to Bill Barrette, an artist and writer, for his thoughtful essay. By discussing Fane's long career as an artist in the context of the art world of the last half of the twentieth century, Barrette has brought us a clearer understanding of the artist's sources and new insights into his art. Also, a special thanks goes to Elaine Koss for her editing.

At the University of Richmond, our special appreciation goes to Dr. William E. Cooper, President; Dr. June R. Aprille, Provost and Vice President for Academic Affairs; and Dr. Andrew F. Newcomb, Acting Dean of the School of Arts and Sciences, for their continuing guidance and support of the University Museums, comprising the Marsh Art Gallery, the Joel and Lila Harnett Print Study Center, and the Lora Robins Gallery of Design from Nature. As always, we give thanks to the staff of the University Museums for their steadfast involvement.

We give thanks to the Muscarelle Museum of Art, The College of William and Mary, especially to Bonnie G. Kelm, Director, and her staff, for their support of this collaboration between our two institutions.

Finally, we acknowledge the generous support of The Richard Florsheim Art Fund, The Cowles Charitable Trust, and the University's Cultural Affairs Committee in making this exhibition and catalogue possible.

RICHARD WALLER
Executive Director
University of Richmond Museums

I measure my song,

measure the sources of my song,

measure me, measure

my forces

— Charles Olsen, *The Maximus Poems*, vol. 1

MENTORS, MACHINES, AND MODERNISMS: SOME THOUGHTS ON THE ART OF LAWRENCE FANE

Lawrence Fane is very careful and articulate when he speaks, but he is not the type of artist given to belaboring a studio visitor with explanations or justifications of his work, and so — even though I have been a frequent visitor to his studio over the years — I was not particularly well informed about the significant details of his development as an artist. Once asked to write about his work for this catalogue, I realized that it would be necessary to interview him at some length. Two long interviews were undertaken: one in September 2001 in Vermont, and the other three months later at his New York studio. There were numerous telephone conversations as well. (All quotes from the artist are from these discussions.) Through this process I learned many things about my friend that I never knew.

I have long been fascinated by how a person decides to become an artist and the path he or she chooses to realize that goal. What impressed me during these interviews were the details of Fane's training as a sculptor in the late 1950s and early 1960s, and how fundamentally different it was from the training I received in New York just a decade later. Clearly a major shift occurred during this time in the way the practice of art was transmitted from one generation to the next. One could say that the period was a hinge moment between Modernist and Postmodernist attitudes toward art education and practice. Today, colleges, art schools, and universities all have standardized curricula for their studio art programs, and it is rare to find a young artist who does not have an M.F.A. This type of art education is so commonplace that few would question its underlying assumptions. But, as we shall see, this was not always the case, and in order to appreciate Fane's choices and achievements as an artist, it is important to know something of his training and the process by which he arrived at the values that are embodied in his work.

In a 1963 article called "What's Wrong with U.S. Art Schools?," the artist and New York Studio School founder Mercedes Matter (1913-2001) served up an indictment of the then-current trend in art education to incorporate studio art programs into four-year liberal arts curricula. Matter was advocating "slow art," the "painfully slow education of the senses . . that took years of schooling as well as a lifelong effort," — something that she believed could not be realized within the framework of a four-year program of study that included courses in the humanities. She argued, with thinly veiled disdain, for the neo-Dada of Marcel Duchamp (1887-1968) and the emerging Pop art, that the basis of art education is

the continuity of work in a studio. Take this away and the art has been taken out of the education, and the art school becomes ready-made for the Ready-Made. The one ballast conceivably available to a student, that of a deep immersion in his own work, carefully is denied him. He is cast into the arena to deal with art and history, at best, on an intellectual level. Today, it is possible for a student to go through art school and gain an acute perception of "what is going on," a fairly intelligent grasp of the situation, and yet have never departed a single step from his original naiveté of vision. In old fashioned language, he never will have "learned to draw." His eye and his hand will have remained as puerile as his intellect will have become sophisticated. The irony is that this does not leave him ill-equipped for making the scene.[1]

I would say that this is a pretty fair description of the art education I received in New York in the late 1960s. In defense, I would point out that the late sixties *were* a time of cultural revolution in America, which, in its aesthetic dimension, influenced not only painting and sculpture but the worlds of music, dance, theater, and film. To be overly concerned with the niceties of tradition at such a time seemed to a young art student to be an untenable position. However, some years later I became aware that my education during this time, as exciting and utopian as it may have seemed, had left me with many ideas but with few practical skills with which to express them. When asked what my art school education was like, I sometimes describe it as "graduating with honors as a painting major without learning how to stretch a canvas." It just wasn't done. Much time and effort would later be required to learn skills on my own that could have more easily and effectively been acquired in art school. Reading Matter's essay brought these issues back into focus, as I realized to what extent our educations had unwittingly placed Fane and me on different sides of the Postmodernist barricades and how, ironically, we had both struggled in opposite ways to free ourselves from the constraints and limitations of our educational choices.

There is little doubt, however, that at the time Matter's 1963 essay appeared, it would have been perceived as hopelessly reactionary. The Pop artists had just had their first exhibitions in New York and Los Angeles, and Minimalism and Conceptualism were in the early stages of what would become a radical critique and redefinition of traditional painting and sculpture by the late 60s. Duchamp's notion of reducing "the idea of aesthetic consideration to the choice of the mind, not to the ability or cleverness of the hand"[2] would have seemed to have won the day. However, Matter's perception of what may have been lost in the bargain still seems hauntingly prescient today: "As values became indistinct, the school of fine arts lost its uncompromising position and more easily succumbed to the general order of things in America, so that instead of an Eakins as president of an academy we now have public-relations experts throughout." At the time this article was written, Fane was thirty years old and just coming to the end of his own long period of training as an artist, about to take up a teaching position at the Rhode Island School of Design. For Fane, the slow process of training the eye, hand, and mind began at Harvard in 1951 and ended at the American Academy in Rome in 1963. One imagines that Ms. Matter would have approved.

KANSAS CITY

Lawrence Fane was born in 1933 in Kansas City, Missouri. As a child he had a lively interest in drawing, and in grade school was considered the class artist. His parents encouraged his drawing, to a certain degree, and from the time he was eight years old until the time he left for college, Fane took drawing classes from various local teachers. He was the type of child who, when taken to a ball game by his father, would spend his time sketching the game. His parents were sufficiently impressed by their young son's drawing ability to arrange — through their rabbi, a mutual friend — an audience with Thomas Hart Benton (1889-1975), the famous painter, muralist, and teacher of Jackson Pollock (1912-1956). Of his encounter with Benton, Fane recalls

He was devastating. He said, "this is just kid's art, children can do this stuff." He said to me, "You have to learn to draw. Look at my drawings. I can draw an Indian and you know what tribe he is from." He showed me all these drawings and said "if you want to be an artist, don't touch paint until you have drawn for four more years and become a master of drawing." It was absolutely horrifying. I stopped doing anything, I couldn't go to museums; it was very debilitating. Then I thought later, "He doesn't draw very well either." But he did have a tremendous power over me.

In spite of Benton's harsh judgment, Fane went on to regain his natural love for and obsession with drawing, but the idea that one must be a good draftsman in order to be an artist stayed with him. Fane's parents were crestfallen by Benton's reaction, but in a way were also relieved "because Benton was considered a bohemian and nobody wanted their children to emulate him, he wore plaid shirts with a necktie and swore."

BOSTON AND GLOUCESTER

When it came time for Fane to go to college, there seemed to be no question that he would become a doctor, following the example of a family friend and mentor. In 1951 he enrolled at Harvard in a premedical program. While there, he continued to be interested in drawing, but had the idea, dimly recalling the traumatic Benton incident, that "if I couldn't draw like Leonardo da Vinci, I couldn't be an artist." He did take one drawing and sculpture course with the artist George Demetrios (1896-1974) the last year of college, and it was a life-changing experience for the young student and "an extraordinary revelation." At that point Fane wanted to go to art school, but hesitated because it seemed "not practical, and I was sure I would be destined to a life of poverty." Fane graduated from Harvard in 1955 with a degree in science and psychology and was accepted by George Washington Medical School in Saint Louis to study to become a surgeon. He ended up attending medical school for "about five days, maybe a week." Arriving at school with his sculpture equipment instead of science books, he and a girlfriend set up a studio in a rented room, hired a model, and started drawing. "It dawned on me then that I liked only women and drawing. So I went to the dean and said that I was leaving medical school. It was the first time that I lost my shyness."

At that point Fane, decided to take his chances on a life dedicated to art and enrolled in the School of the Museum of Fine Arts, Boston. There he studied for a year while continuing to take drawing classes with Demetrios, who was at that time teaching a class at the Institute of Contemporary Art in Boston. The chemistry between Fane and Demetrios was right, the older artist realizing that Fane "had the bug" and was ready to commit himself to the discipline of becoming a sculptor. After leaving the School of the Museum of Fine Arts in 1957, the young artist rented a studio in Boston with Demetrios's son Aris, and they organized a little group school for "wealthy ladies from the North Shore" who the elder Demetrios knew. The students would get instruction from Fane and Aris, and once a week George Demetrios would give critiques. During the next two years of intensive work, Fane's role evolved from that of student to studio apprentice to protégé of the older sculptor. The range of skills acquired at this time was considerable and included stone and wood carving, modeling in clay and plaster, bronze casting, mold making, and even the making of anatomical *écorché* sculptures. These sculptures were figure studies that showed musculature beneath the skin in accurate, scientific detail.

In 1958 Fane and Aris Demetrios accompanied George Demetrios to a foundry in Florence, Italy, to assist in the bronze casting of a large commissioned work of Moses. This necessitated enlarging a five-foot plaster to an eighteen-foot clay model, from which a mold was taken for the bronze cast. Fane recalls that "during that time he [George Demetrios] arranged to have us work in a marble-carving shop, and there we learned how to carve marble and use a pointing machine to reproduce sculptures." The use of a pointing machine is a rare skill nowadays, to say the least; however, it was the common and preferred technique for mechanically transferring plaster models into marble sculptures in the nineteenth-century academic tradition. One might think of it as a kind of camera lucida for sculptors. Fane bought one while in Italy, and years later in New York, the eminent art historian H. W. Janson (1913-1982) heard that Fane had such a device. Never having seen a pointing machine, Janson made a special trip to Fane's studio to see it.

Fane continued working as an assistant to Demetrios until 1960, when, with Demetrios's encouragement and support, he applied for and received the Rome Prize to study sculpture at the American Academy in Rome. The fellowship was renewed in 1961 and 1962, and the three years Fane spent refining his skills in Rome were to be an important coda to the long years spent in the process of "educating the senses." Before considering the Rome period, however, a digression on George Demetrios is in order, for there is no doubt that he was the central influence on Fane's development as an artist.

GEORGE DEMETRIOS

Demetrios was born in Greece in 1896 and at age sixteen came to study at the Pennsylvania Academy of the Fine Arts with the sculptor Charles Grafly (1862-1929). Grafly, an academic "monument" sculptor, headed the sculpture department at the same time that Thomas Eakins (1844-1916) was in charge of the painting department. During his years of study there, Demetrios developed a close father-son relationship with Grafly and eventually became his protégé. With the older sculptor's support, the young artist was sent to Paris to finish his studies at the École des Beaux-Arts; he was, for a time, the studio assistant of the well-known French academic sculptor Emile-Antoine Bourdelle (1861-1929), who in turn had been the studio assistant of Auguste Rodin (1840-1917). Besides sculpture, Demetrios studied drawing and was attracted to Rodin's "quick pose style," which was considered quite radical for the time. After finishing his studies, Demetrios went back to America to take a position at the School of the Museum of Fine Arts in Boston, from which he was eventually ostracized because his drawing style seemed insufficiently academic. He had a studio in Gloucester (which he had inherited from Grafly) and taught drawing and sculpture to students privately. Although portraits and commissions came his way, the combination of his irascible temperament with his artistically reclusive nature contributed to the lack of wide recognition.

When Fane became an apprentice to Demetrios in 1957, the young artist was connecting himself to a tradition of study that, despite the many challenges of Modernism, had remained essentially unchanged since the nineteenth century. This tradition — with a long period of dependence on a master followed by a kind of familial relationship, and then placement in a position of the academic hierarchy — was a central part of the academic system of education. Already creaky since the advent of the Bauhaus in the 1920s, the system began to break down after the rapid cultural changes following World War II. By the early 1960s, this type of training was nearly extinct as an option available to a young artist, and it was quite an anomaly that Fane was able to pursue it. Needless to say, it would be difficult, if not impossible, to duplicate this kind of education today.[3]

What kind of tradition was being handed down in this slow and intense apprenticeship, and what was the training like? Learning to draw well, as we have seen, was the chief motivating factor in Fane's search for a teacher. "I had this idea, which I have since rejected, that you couldn't be an artist until you drew in a grand way. . . You had to earn your right to go beyond that." Drawing was at the core of the Academic tradition, with students required to spend years of rigorous effort drawing from casts and the model. Fane was dissatisfied with the drawing classes given at the School of the Fine Arts and, after an initial class with Demetrios, he realized that "this man really had something to teach me." For three years Fane studied drawing, portraiture, anatomy, and sculpture with him, "very much in the tradition of the French Academy." Fane recalls that Demetrios's idols

were Greek sculpture and Rodin. His drawing

method came from Rodin in the sense that Demetrios believed in very fast drawing where you would capture the gesture. We would, every once in a while, at the end of the day, do a long drawing that would last a half hour or more. But for the most part we would draw very fast. He would always quote Leonardo da Vinci: "You should be able to draw a man falling out of a fifth-story window and finish the drawing before he hits the ground, and it should be a very good likeness." He would circulate the room and make great slashing corrections on the drawings. . . It was a tremendously exciting atmosphere for learning. On a deeper level, though, I realized that there were certain, you might call them, truths about the structure of the human figure that all of the great figurative traditions have understood — African, Romanesque, Greek obviously: structural things like movements of the leg that make the figure stand up, even if they are quite exaggerated. What I got from him was these basic truths that I still continue to find. For instance, there is a Cubist head by Picasso [1881-1973] at MoMA made in many facets, and I was realizing a couple of years ago that it is very symmetrical, everything is balanced in a way that he [Demetrios] would have called correct. By making this balanced structural framework on which to hang the rest, the Cubist invention takes on an even richer formal vocabulary.

But, Fane recalls, "Demetrios didn't appreciate Picasso's art at all. . . He just didn't understand it, and, as it can be for many artists, it can be a threat, for Picasso drew like an angel." The threat of Picasso's and other Modernists' assault on academic tradition was very real to an artist of Demetrios's generation and training, but it was not so for Fane, who was developing an interest in abstraction. One artist whom Fane and his teacher could agree on was Constantin Brancusi (1876-1957), who had "earned his right" to his abstractions after a thorough training as an academic sculptor in Romania. The notion of earning one's right to make abstract art was very much part of a discourse around abstraction that endured until the 1960s but is rarely heard today. In a way, it recalls Goethe's dictum "What you have inherited from your fathers you must earn in order to possess." For Fane, Brancusi would become an important model during his stay in Rome and remain so all his life. Although out of sync with many of his peers, Fane felt that his challenge as a young artist was not unlike Brancusi's: to find a way to reconcile the classical academic figural tradition with his growing interest in abstraction. He wanted to push toward abstraction but without totally giving up allusion to the figure. This cat-and-mouse game between the perceived freedom of abstraction and more tradition-bound figuration has, with varying degrees of intensity, preoccupied artists throughout the century. At the same time, other artists of Fane's generation, whose training was already rooted in Modernist abstraction, followed the lead of art critic Clement Greenberg (1909-1994) who favored a more radical Postmodern reevaluation of sculpture that sought to eliminate all subject matter, illusion, and reference to the self — in effect reducing sculpture to its most basic formal constituents. Ultimately, Fane would devote a large part of his career to working the classical Modernist side of this issue, trying to find a comfortable balance between abstraction and figuration.

By the time Fane left for Rome in 1960, he had already started moving in the direction of abstraction and, as we shall see, the time in Rome would be key to establishing the foundations for his work far away from the art centers of the United States and the influence of his former teacher. Before leaving, he paid a visit to the sculptor Paul Manship (1885-1966), who lived in Gloucester and had given him a recommendation for the Rome Prize.

> I showed him photos of my work and he said, "This stuff is terrible; if I had known you were going to go in this direction I would have tried to veto you from that place," and then he said to me, "This idea of originality, that's ridiculous, the great artists were the Greeks and the Chinese, and if you combine those two you will be a great artist, this other stuff is silly."

There is something almost comical about this story that brings to mind the famous scene in the movie *The Graduate* where Dustin Hoffman is given the dubious advice from a loutish relative at a party that the surest way to success lies in the direction of "plastic." The fact that Fane was able to find the rebuff amusing also indicates the considerable distance traveled since the Benton critique and demonstrates that one of the most useful attributes a young artist needs to develop is a thick skin. On another level, though, Manship's response is an interesting index to the extent that artists like Manship and Demetrios felt threatened by the erosion of the academic values on which their work was based. It is perhaps too easy to ridicule Manship's remarks today, but in retrospect, one must ask whether his advice was any less useful than Greenberg's pontification of the period that "content is to be dissolved so completely into form that the work of art or literature cannot be reduced in whole or in part to anything not itself."[4] Fane would have to find his own way of negotiating the line between abstraction and figuration.

ROME

In the fall of 1960 Fane left for Rome. He had been in Italy the year before, working in Florence with Demetrios, but the prospect of an extended stay free from the constraints of his sometimes overbearing teacher had a liberating effect on the young artist's work. At the same time, Fane was to establish strong links to the art and landscape of Italy, links that have remained important sources in his work.

I got a Rome Prize just out of art school, and it was sort of like my graduate school. It was the first time I got to work on my own. It was very important because my work at that time had been highly programmed in terms of looking at the human figure as an anatomical object, and I was very good at anatomy. We [Fane and Aris Demetrios] were real groupies at that time, and I must say, it cut us off from what was happening in the art world completely. When I got to Italy I began to meet people who were more involved with a freer approach to making art, and as a result, my work became more biomorphic and abstract.

Among the artists that Fane encountered during his residency at the Academy were the sculptors Anthony Padovano, Philip Pavia, James Wines, Calvin Albert, Gilbert Franklin, Phillip Grausman, Elbert Weinberg (1928-1991), and Isamu Noguchi (1904-1988); the painters Bernard Chaet, Robert Birmelin, and James Brooks (1906-1992); and the architects Michael Graves and Wayne Taylor. Fane recalls,

Of all the people at the Academy, the person who was the most progressive in the way he talked about art was Calvin Albert. I remember a conversation with him where I said that I was at the point where "I can make anything I can imagine," and what he said was, "What you want to do is get to the point of making anything you can't imagine." I have to say, it made an impression on me.

The lively give-and-take provided by his new environment proved stimulating for Fane. "They gave me a studio and I did sculptures that were kind of abstracted figures. I also began working in concrete as a way of modeling in a permanent material. My work at first was more stylized, still quite retrograde, like that of artists I admired at the time, such as Ernst Barlach [1870-1938], Henry Moore [1898-1986], Georg Kolbe [1877-1947], Marino Marini [1901-1980], and Giacomo Manzu [1908-1991]," artists who were working in a style combining abstraction and figuration who had become popular in the thirties. "What I was doing made sense within the context of the people being chosen for the Academy, who were just on the verge of a certain modernism and abstraction, and it made sense in Rome. You didn't see Arte Povera in the galleries of Rome at that time."

However, a significant change of direction took place in June 1962, when Fane traveled to Spoleto to see the *Sculptures in the City* exhibition for which fifty sculptors had been commissioned to install work throughout the city as part of Gian-Carlo Menotti's Festival of Two Worlds at Spoleto. Fane encountered David Smith's exhibition of large-scale welded steel sculptures, dramatically installed in the ancient Roman amphitheater of the town. Smith (1906-1965) had been lured to Italy by Menotti's promise to provide the artist free reign of a recently abandoned railway-car factory in the town of Voltri, near Genoa. A further enticement had been Menotti's offer to dedicate an opera to Smith's daughters. A crew of metalworker assistants was placed at Smith's disposal, and the artist was given carte blanche to work undisturbed for a month. Within the month, the proposed two works for the festival stretched in number to twenty-six. The popular image of Smith as a mythic fusion of Paul Bunyan and Vulcan, beating the iron relics of the industrial age into lyrical sculptures in a surge of creative frenzy, had a great appeal at the time, and the theatrical installation of the pieces made it difficult not to see Smith's heroic gesture in operatic terms — passionate, monumental, and tragic. The installation caused a sensation in Italy, and the enthusiastic reception of the work invigorated Smith during a time when Abstract Expressionism was entering a period of decline in the United States, a time when interest in another artist working in a "factory" — Andy Warhol (1928-1987) — was supplanting Abstract Expressionism's claim to center stage. The resulting Voltri series is among the most impressive of Smith's late works and served as a capstone to a career that was cut short by a fatal auto accident three years later.

Fane had been slightly aware of Smith's work from photographs before coming to Rome but was not overly sympathetic to it. This view was to change after seeing the works in

Spoleto; they would be, for Fane, "the most jarring event of my time in Rome, hugely impressive and not like anything else there. It changed my way of looking at things and, most of all, made me very much want to learn how to weld. It also made me question the foundations of what I was doing." He felt challenged by the older artist's work — not so much by the vocabulary of the forms but by the enormous possibilities offered by working with welded and forged steel. Perhaps he sensed, as Smith had earlier said, that metal itself possesses little art history, and that an artist could be freer to invent using less traditional materials and techniques. Fane quickly set to work learning how to weld from the sculptor Tony Padovano and began to offer his services at a local foundry in order to learn every step of the bronze-casting and bronze-finishing process, including welding. On his own, he began to experiment with forging and, with the help of an architectural colleague at the Academy, he learned to work with cement and concrete.

Fane had also been impressed by the innovative use of steel and concrete in the buildings of the Italian architect Pier Luigi Nervi (1891-1979), whose architecture was much discussed in Rome at this time, and saw possibilities for using this combination of materials for his own work. By combining steel and concrete, Fane wanted to suggest the "softness of flesh with the hardness of bone" in a series of sensuous abstracted figure sculptures begun at this time and continued after his return to America. Working in steel and concrete also allowed the artist to make sculpture on a larger scale and to work in a freer and more direct way, eliminating the need to enlarge and cast his work. Steel and concrete are normally associated with rough industrial fabrication, but it was not this aspect of the materials that most appealed to Fane. He went to considerable lengths to transform the quality of the concrete he used to a more classically elegant finish by first adding black marble chips and dust and then grinding and polishing the surface so that the concrete resembled granite. His ability to manipulate and transform humble materials, using them in unexpected ways, is characteristic of much of his sculpture.

Fane's sources of influence were undergoing a change also. Early Renaissance, Romanesque, and Pre-Columbian art contributed to his thinking about form. He found Pre-Columbian art (which he had seen for the first time at a large exhibition in Rome) particularly impressive, and it influenced his aesthetic approach to his steel and concrete works. The time in Rome was important to Fane on a personal level as well, for it was there that he met Diana Gilmore, the woman he would marry soon after returning to the United States.

RHODE ISLAND

As we have seen, Fane's path as an artist had begun and developed outside the orbit of the

New York art scene. By his own admission he "was isolated and in my own world" during his training in Boston, Gloucester, and Rome. Furthermore, when he arrived to join the faculty at the Rhode Island School of Design in 1963, Providence, too, was somewhat of a cultural and artistic backwater. However, the three years spent teaching there gave him time to refine his work before moving to New York, his goal since leaving Rome. "I remember something Jim Brooks said to me in Rome. He said, 'going to New York is very important because, not only do you see the work, but you start running into these artists, and you find out that they are very smart in spite of what you may have thought, so that's why you have to be there,' and he was right." In 1966 Fane secured a job teaching sculpture at Queens College, and he and his wife and their infant son moved to New York. New York in the late sixties was a hotbed of art activity, yet the timing was far from ideal for an artist with Fane's background and sensibility hoping to find a receptive audience.

NEW YORK

Fane was not fully aware of it, but he was entering the fray of the New York art scene exactly at the time that the very skills he had spent so long mastering were in the process of being banished by a generation of young Minimalist artists. As Anne Rorimer points out in her book on the period,[5]

The reappraisal directed towards sculpture's material and formal attributes at the outset of the 1960s by Tony Smith (1912-1980), Donald Judd (1928-1994), Carl Andre (b. 1935), Sol LeWitt (b. 1928), Robert Morris (b. 1931), Richard Serra (b. 1939), and Eva Hesse (1936-1970) — all living in New York or its vicinity — laid the foundations for the ensuing demise of sculpture's long-held three-dimensional materiality. Often characterized by the terms Minimal or Post-Minimal because of their pared-down, non-referential qualities, works by these artists reevaluated accepted formulations of sculptural materiality They detour from the normally traveled routes of sculptural production in order to protect themselves against the display of decision-making processes, skillful workmanship, or subjective expressiveness on the part of the artist.

One must also include the artist Dan Flavin (1933-1996) in this list, whose work with fluorescent light was very much a part of the dematerialization of sculpture in the sixties.

It should be underscored that most of the artists mentioned above had been initially trained as painters. Many of them viewed a move into the arena of sculpture as an opportunity to apply to three-dimensional work the reductivist theories that had previously been associated with painting and were, by the mid-sixties, felt to be at an impasse. Their strategies were developed in opposition to traditional sculptural practice, and in this respect their lack of knowledge and training in its materials and techniques could be considered an advantage of sorts, for they had nothing to un-learn. Unlike Fane, they had not invested years in acquiring the skills traditionally associated with sculpture. As a result, once demand for their work increased, most of these artists had little choice but to resort to professional fabrication to have their ideas realized. This is not to criticize the practice of fabrication, but to draw a distinction between the different ways it has been used. Traditionally trained sculptors — especially those involved in large-scale architectural commissions — have often relied upon foundries to have their works enlarged or cast. But there is a fundamental difference between this type of practice, where the artist exerts a certain control of the process, and that of the Minimalists and Conceptualists, where the use of industrial fabrication was part of a philosophy of rejection of the handmade, along with the subjective decision-making process that it implied.[6]

For an artist like Fane — whose work was so firmly rooted in drawing, structural "truths" derived from the study of anatomy, skilled workmanship, and the appreciation and mastery of the diverse traditions that flow into and inform classical Modernist sculpture — the appeal of the new Minimalist and Conceptualist orthodoxy was, well, "minimal." He could not imagine "dictating pieces for others to make," his one experiment in that direction "turned out to be a disaster." His is an art to which the hand and an intuitive creative process are central, and they take precedence over any overriding theoretical strategies. Reflecting on the effect of the late sixties art scene on his work, Fane responds,

> You know, I have never changed very quickly; things build one on top of another . . . I wasn't fighting against things, but my work did evolve. I never said, "this is of the past, I am not doing this anymore," because it seemed to come from another place — within me — so the evolution was quite slow, and the art world kept moving quite fast, and I saw things go up and down, and I kept going horizontally.

This is not to say that Fane was singular in his approach to sculpture. There were many artists of similar disposition working in New York in the 1960s; they just were not getting much attention in the pages of *Artforum,* the journal that was the main broker of reputations and definer of the artistically correct for much of the 1960s and 1970s. The artist H. C. Westermann (1922-1981) comes to mind as an example of a sculptor whose work reflected an obsession with craft and the handmade. Westermann railed against everything that was shoddy and mass-produced in postwar America, but it was not until very recently, twenty years after the artist's death, that his work was acknowledged as "deserving to be rated as one of the great American talents and should have been long ago."[7] Two artists for whom Fane felt a particular affinity were the sculptors Edward Higgins and Lee Bontecou, both represented by the Leo Castelli Gallery. Higgins, whose work was made of steel plates and pipes with sections of plaster, had an obvious appeal to Fane from a formal point of view, while Bontecou's metal and cloth wall reliefs — with their menacing reference to parts of the body and their dark psychological undercurrents — also made a strong impression. Both artists, but especially Bontecou, had promising career starts in the early 1960s, but by the end of the decade had been eclipsed by artists whose work had been purged of any figurative allusion.

Fane secured representation from the Virginia Zabriskie Gallery for his first one-person show in 1969, where he exhibited steel and concrete works. Reviewing the exhibition for *The New York Times*, Hilton Kramer acknowledged Fane's "considerable talent for a mode of semiabstract figurative sculpture not much pursued these days by the younger generation. He is certainly a pro in his chosen style, and occasionally — I think especially in the small polished bronze, 'Leaning Torso' (1968) — produces a really eloquent piece." The review was decent enough "to pin on the gallery bulletin board" but not sufficiently enthusiastic to bring collectors to the show. In other words, there were some sales, but commercial interest was not strong enough to convince Fane's dealer to do more than include him in group shows in the early seventies. In fairness to the dealer, it should be pointed out that this would have been an extremely difficult

time to introduce a young sculptor whose work was linked so strongly to the classical Modernist tradition. Zabriskie's stable included a number of sculptors whose work was aesthetically comparable to Fane's, but they were older and more established in their careers and therefore better positioned to weather the downturn of interest in their style of sculpture.

THE GLOUCESTER SERIES

In the mid-1970s, Fane changed his affiliation from Zabriskie Gallery to the Marilyn Pearl Gallery on 57th Street, beginning an association that would continue until the late 1980s. Reception to his work gradually improved, and during the course of his tenure he had four one-person shows and was included in a number of group exhibitions. Altogether, the early seventies were a period of experimentation and growth for Fane, and it is worth considering the work at that time in some detail as the formal and technical innovations he introduced then continued and evolved over the next twenty years.

On the one hand, Fane's use of concrete in combination with steel diminished, as well as the erotically charged figurative aspect of the work. What emerged were welded and forged steel works that had, as their source of inspiration, the rock formations of the quarries in Gloucester that Fane drew during his summers there. Formally, the language of the Gloucester series is considerably more abstract than that of the 1960s work; with abstraction, the sensualized torsos gave way to a more subtle and diffused merging of figure and landscape. In this context we are reminded of the work of Arthur Dove (1880-1946), and, significantly, Fane had a black-and-white reproduction of the Dove painting *Arrangement in Form 1* pinned to his studio wall for many years. Fane also made a drawing after an Aaron Siskind (1903-1991) photograph, which, like the Dove work, was an abstracted arrangement of rock forms precariously balanced one on top of the other.

There is another American Modernist whose work is geographically as well as spiritually close to Fane's Gloucester sculptures, and that is Marsden Hartley (1877-1943). In the 1920s and 1930s Hartley made a series of landscape paintings sometimes referred to as the Dogtown series, after the section in Gloucester where they were painted. The area is known for strange geologic outcroppings that have the appearance of being arranged in a manner not unlike the dolmens of Brittany. The totemic aspect of these formations attracted Hartley and were the basis of many of the Dogtown paintings. Fane knew the Dogtown area intimately from his years studying with Demetrios, and he also knew and admired Hartley's work. In fact, Fane's bas-relief from the mid-seventies, *Whale's Jaw,* was modeled from the very rock formation of the same name that Hartley had used as the central motif in one of his Dogtown paintings, and the relief can be considered an homage to the

older artist.[8] A number of works from the Gloucester series refer to dolmens in their titles, underscoring the reading of the stony landscape as a locus for a kind of prehistoric ritual. The evocation of transcendent primal forces and their embodiment in the landscape is strong in Fane's work of the seventies, and links him with a tradition of artists inspired by Gloucester. This includes not only artists like Hartley and Stuart Davis (1894-1964), but also the poet Charles Olsen (1910-1970), whose masterwork, *The Maximus Poems,* was a career-long meditation on the cosmos, with Gloucester as its mythological center.

Fane's Gloucester sculptures developed in three discrete phases beginning in the early 1970s and extending until the early 1990s. The earliest phase is the most abstract and is closely derived from the quarry drawings. Many of the bas-reliefs done at this time are small in scale and are created in plaster and cast in bronze. At times the forms have an overlay of figurative association, but this quality is muted compared to the more aggressive figuration of the work that followed. In the mid-seventies, Fane began working in steel, and the sculptures became larger and more complicated. There was a merging of landscape, human, and tool forms as the artist began to incorporate found industrial elements in his work. This addition sometimes gave an odd mechanical feel to the work, and the juxtaposition of the human and the mechanical can sometimes be quite shocking, in a manner reminiscent of the erotic machine-drawings of

Francis Picabia (1879-1953).[9] Fane remarks that at the time he was especially taken with the work of the little-known Renaissance sculptor Agostino di Duccio (1418- after 1481), whose bas-reliefs he had earlier traveled to Rimini, Italy, to see. "His work had a landscape quality, and the feeling of sheer cloth covering the figure had a big effect on the steel pieces." The last phase of the Gloucester series occurred in the late 1980s and early 1990s, when Fane began to experiment with coloring the metal with increasingly elaborate patinas. The inspiration was Japanese landscape painting, and, while formally close to his previous work, the use of vivid color had a flattening effect on the forms as well as a surprising and sometimes gravity-defying effect.

Much of the sculpture of the 1970s is made from forged and welded steel, darkened to a dark gray or black patina to reinforce the impression that the works are cast. The welds are not visible, and the complex shapes and the intricate interior joining involved in the construction would be considered a tour de force if the viewer were able to appreciate fully how it was done. The pieces are hollow, partly for practical reasons and partly in emulation of Chinese and Renaissance bronzes. The deceptiveness implied by their hollowness at first pleased Fane but over the years became problematic for him and was another reason he began to consider wood as an alternative medium.

Beginning in the mid-1970s, many of the Gloucester sculptures of welded and forged steel contained reworked elements from automobile bumpers and other found industrial forms, such as tools. Originally Fane forged the complex irregularly curved shapes that make up part of these works, but after realizing that these forms could more efficiently be created by reusing sections of automobile bumpers, he developed a technique by which he would cut out the section that he needed, transform and adjust its surface and shape, and then weld it into a larger structure. Like so much that happens in art, this discovery occurred by chance when Fane was visiting a junkyard in search of material. He was attracted to a pile of discarded bumpers from the 1950s and 1960s, curvaceous examples of the most exuberant, if nonfunctional, era of American automobile design. I remember visiting one of these places with him in New Jersey, a vast warehouse specializing in used bumpers of every imaginable description. Tangles of fantastic metal shapes glittered in the dimness like relics from the age of the driveway dinosaurs. Fane, who was by that time a connoisseur of bumper typology, made his selection quickly, cash changed hands, and the chrome trophies were unceremoniously dumped into the back of my van for the trip back to Fane's Manhattan studio. There they would be stored until inspiration called them to a higher life as abstract forms incorporated into sculpture.

The use of found or preexisting imagery has been one of the most enduring techniques of modern art since the advent of the Cubist collage. Every generation has its own version of this idea — "appropriation" and "sampling" being only the most recent variations. For a number of artists of Fane's generation, the idea of recycling found objects and integrating them into sculptural assemblages enjoyed a certain vogue and was to be an important precursor of the appropriation of "low" art forms by Pop artists in the 1960s. The "junk" sculptures of Richard Stankiewicz (1922-1983) and Jean Tinguely (1925-1991) come to mind, as well as the constructions of the painter Robert Rauschenberg. However, Fane's work is devoid of Pop sensibility, and there is something significantly different in his reuse of discarded industrial parts that is more usefully contrasted with that of David Smith's Voltri series.

Smith, like Fane, had been born in the Midwest and, although both were from bourgeois families, they identified themselves — on the level of their artistic productions at least — with a blue-collar work ethic. In the summer of 1925, Smith worked in the Studebaker factory in South Bend, Indiana, and, although brief, the experience had a lasting effect on the sculptor. This preassembly line factory experience gave him a taste of skilled manual labor at a time when a worker was expected to master a wide variety of skills after a long apprenticeship — a kind of labor that was all but eliminated by the advent of automation introduced by Henry Ford. In his history of the automobile industry, James J. Flink points out, "Fordism meant that neither physical strength nor the long apprenticeship required for

becoming a competent craftsman were any longer prerequisites for industrial employment. The creativity and experience on the job that had been valued in the craftsman were considered liabilities in the assembly-line worker."[10] In notes on his Voltri experience, Smith describes the empty railway-car factory that had been turned over to him. "Now deserted by automation, these factories were from the handmade days, the 10-, 11-, 12-hour days when working was living. In the new automated plant, the hours are shorter, the man is a machine part. He lives outside the gates only."[11] The tools, machine parts, carts, and even whole workbenches that Smith found and reconfigured into his sculptures have an archaeological and elegiacal air about them; they reflect back to an earlier industrial age and onto what had been lost in this century — the respect for crafts and artisanal skills and traditions, the value of the hand — as America turned from a nation that made things to one that manipulated markets and ideas.

As for Fane, his paternal grandfather had been a tailor in Russia who had come to America in the late nineteenth century. He died when Fane was still a child. The artist eventually inherited the simple tools of his grandfather's trade, some of which he still uses. One suspects that Fane also inherited his grandfather's aptitude for precise hand-labor as well as the modesty inherent in the tailor's art, where the perfection of the final product obscures the evidence of the time and skill that go into its making. Fane's manual skills would later serve to differentiate him from his father, who became a lawyer by following a familiar pattern in the immigration history of this country, where successive generations seek to improve their economic lot through education and white-collar work. For someone of Fane's generation, the choice of pursuing a life of the hand over a life of the mind was unusual, especially considering his obvious intellectual gifts and the resources of his family. Perhaps this helps to explain his choice to accomplish both goals, by first graduating from Harvard in science before taking up his pursuit of sculpture. For Fane, who also had had the direct experience of artisanal labor from the time spent apprenticed to his teacher in Gloucester and Boston and to the stone and metal workers in Italy, the remaking and integration of found machine parts into his sculpture would have more than purely aesthetic connotations. They would also have a psychologically complex resonance.

On one level, we might view both Smith's and Fane's gestures as defiant and self-affirming claims of the autonomy of the hand over the machine. They would not become machine parts — bent into shape by society — they would do the bending, and they were strong and clever enough to do it by themselves with their own hands. What appealed most to Fane about Smith's Voltri sculptures was they "had the trace of the hand in the fabrication — the hand as an expressive tool." By transforming the "ready-made" into the "handmade," both artists would also be issuing a subtle challenge not only to

Duchamp's denigration of the "ability or cleverness of the hand" in the world of art, but to Ford's banishment of "competent craftsmen" from the workplace as well.[12] One could also compare the sincerity of these assertions of the handmade to the more ironic art productions emerging from the assembly line of Warhol's "factory," which operated at full capacity throughout the 1960s and 1970s.

In many other respects, the two artists' sensibilities could not be more different. Smith's Voltri series is large scaled, full of heroic gestures, and raw and immediate in the way that the forms are integrated. The viewer can feel a bit bullied by the scale and rhetorical force of the work. Fane's art is more modestly human in scale, and the forms are slow-cooked and tinkered with until there is only a vestigial presence of their former identities. The attitude of the work is soft-spoken, bemused, and enigmatic. The activity in Smith's sculpture seems to be taking place on the surfaces: welds and tool marks are left as evidence of the strong presence of the artist's will. In contrast, Fane's steel sculptures usually give the impression of complex interior forces pushing up and creating forms from within, and the evidence of his hand is often carefully disguised or erased so as not to call too much attention to itself. For Fane and Smith there are fundamental differences in personality, but they also have much in common: their insistence on retaining control of every aspect of their work, and their respect for the expressive power of the hand.

As we have seen, these characteristics, though admirable, were out of step with the mainstream sculpture scene of the 1960s and 1970s. But the situation changed dramatically in the 1980s as a rapidly rising art market was ushered in by the "voodoo economics" of the Reagan years. Galleries sprang up overnight in SoHo, and, with great entrepreneurial zeal, a younger generation of art dealers chased after the newly wealthy collectors who were eager to buy art like stocks, as investments. Not surprisingly, some of the mega-collectors emerged from the new corporate wealth, such as the now-notorious advertising magnate Charles Saatchi. It was also during this period that most of the major corporations began to form art collections. These developments were not lost on artists, and along with a "neo-Expressionist" return to figuration there was also newly found interest in the appearance of hands-on craftsmanship, as certain artists began to reconsider the financial advantages of having their work cast in bronze editions. Having been banished as an acceptable medium since the 1960s for its preciousness and association with academic art, bronze made a comeback as a material in a big way in the 1980s. Ironically, at this time very few sculptors had any experience with bronze casting and were at a disadvantage when their work was enlarged and cast at local foundries such as Talix in Brewster, New York, or Johnson Atelier in Princeton, New Jersey. Their lack of knowledge of the various steps involved in the preparation, casting, finishing, and patination of bronzes put these artists at the mercy of the foundries, and a kind of tail-wagging-the-dog effect occurred, with the result that much of the bronze work of this period has a similar look and impersonal feel; even though there is a suggestion of the artist's hand at work, it is mostly illusory. Painters such as Willem de Kooning (1904-1997), Jim Dine, and Julian Schnabel even turned to bronze sculpture in order to capitalize on the booming market for corporate commissions by "blue chip" artists. Dine's gargantuan Venuses on the Avenue of the Americas at 53th Street are the best example of this trend at its height.

Fane did benefit somewhat from the new interest afforded to more traditional forms and techniques, for, as economists and politicians of the period were fond of saying, "a rising tide lifts all boats." However, his work did not have the requisite large scale nor did it possess the necessary expressionist hubris so attractive to the corporate mandarins of the late 1980s. Significantly, Fane, who was thoroughly versed in every aspect of bronze production, did relatively little work in bronze in the eighties — his mind and markets were elsewhere.

THE TACCOLA SERIES

In the early 1990s, Fane's work underwent a profound transformation as he became increasingly involved with the study of the drawings and notebooks of a little-known Italian Renaissance artist named Mariano

Taccola (1382 - before 1453). According to Fane's recent study,[13] Taccola was an artist-engineer, quite possibly the first in a category that would later include Leonardo da Vinci (1452-1519). Taccola was also a civil and hydraulic engineer, inventor, and humanist who called himself the "Sienese Archimedes." His drawings of machines, war implements, and other inventions were carefully organized into bound notebooks that were widely distributed throughout Europe and may have served as models for Leonardo's own notebooks. Taccola's drawings vanished from sight and from general interest soon after his death, and his work is very little known or appreciated today even among scholars of the Renaissance.

Fane's long and ongoing study of Taccola — one might term it an obsession — is so unusual that it would not be an exaggeration to view this study as the artist's second apprenticeship. His first apprenticeship, to Demetrios, can be thought of as an apprenticeship of the hand — as Fane acquired the formidable skills with which he could make anything he could imagine. The problem with this apprenticeship was that the aesthetic tradition that those skills were meant to serve was not truly viable for him; he needed to spend the next thirty years searching for a vision that encompassed enough to match his talents and, at the same time, balance his respect for the past with the imperatives of the present. Fane's second apprenticeship, with Taccola, was an apprenticeship of the imagination and did not involve the acquisition of techniques and skills,

but instead resulted in a dramatic liberation of his own way of thinking and seeing. It opened up a new world for him, a world that had been there all along but had been slightly beyond his grasp. Fane's encounter with Taccola was "like finding a distant ancestor and discovering that he was part of a tradition that I didn't understand before." It was a tradition in which the artist could finally feel at home.

By the early 1990s, Fane had been growing dissatisfied with the properties of his metal sculptures. Their hollowness began to bother him, and he also realized that after going to great lengths to add color to the surface, the end result was too often a beautiful but contradictory sense of weight, mass, and gravity. Fane was ripe for a new source of inspiration, and it came to him gradually in 1992, when an art historian colleague of his at Queens College brought his attention to the drawings of Taccola. He was able to borrow a book of facsimile drawings for one night and made his own drawings from them. The appeal and influence of Taccola's drawing style was immediate, and it first had an effect on Fane's own drawing. Before learning of Taccola, Fane remarks, "I never really thought of the drawings I made as independent works for anyone else to see. And just in the last couple of years, I found that people do seem to be interested in looking at them. So they are becoming works on their own and are certainly influenced by the nature of Taccola's sketchbooks." Fane was not able to see examples of Taccola's work again until 1993 when he had the opportunity to accompany his wife, an art historian, to the Getty Research Institute in Los Angeles, where she had a fellowship. The Fanes stayed in California for a year, and during that time, the artist had unfettered access to facsimiles of Taccola's sketchbooks. Fane says that the year at the Getty "was a very important year, I almost wish that it had occurred twenty-five years earlier. It is what I see as the work for which I would like to be remembered." During that year Fane realized that Taccola's work was having a profound effect on his own, not only on his drawing, but on his conception of sculpture as well. "It is not that my work changed so dramatically, but I began to see it in a different way, and that is one of the most important kinds of influences."

When the Fanes arrived in Los Angeles, the artist quickly set himself the task of renting and outfitting a studio for himself and setting to work on a wood piece that he had begun during the summer and felt was quite promising. He had made wood sculptures from time to time but "they were much like the steel pieces — they were quite refined, but they didn't have the sense of using wood freely." Fane was now ready to understand the lessons of Taccola, and a new freedom, exuberance, and ease of construction began to emerge.

The forms of the earlier steel pieces were liberated as he began to patch wood elements together, in a way not possible before, and the result was that a new quality of informality, one that he had been trying for years to achieve, entered the work. The pieces were meant to look as if they just somehow happened. "This is what I had been pushing for. It was very important to me that these things appeared as almost dumb objects, that they looked as if they have a right to exist and they come from some other world and that they don't look like they have been labored over." Contributing to his sense of freedom was the fact that Fane was separated from the tools and conveniences of his studio in New York. In Los Angeles his choices were limited, and this also had a salutary effect on his work, forcing him to simplify his procedures. The surfaces of the new work underwent a change at this time; they were not applied and fussed over as before, but were left in a much rougher state, revealing the process by which they were made. Color, which had been such a struggle with the steel pieces, found a more receptive surface in the rough-cut wood, and a whole new palette of warm reds, ochres, browns, and light greens developed that were not possible before.

In more recent work, Fane returned to one of his first loves — concrete — but this time the surface is left in its raw state, showing the marks of the mold, not elegantly finished and polished as before. The combination of concrete and wood adds to the feeling of ungainly charm that many of the pieces seem to have, and the effect can be disarming. But propelling all the technical innovations of the work done in California was the encounter with Taccola, and the ideas expressed in his engineering drawings. Fane recalls, "It clicked, there is no question about that. I was really ready for it. I think that if I had seen those drawings some years before I wouldn't have been ready to appreciate him on that level."

Formally, much of the work of the Taccola series gives the strong suggestion of implements of some sort, purposeful and useful in ways that elude our comprehension. There is a strong sense of the vestigial about the work, and at times a humorous feeling insinuates itself in a way that is unlike anything in the artist's previous work. The viewer struggles to find a proper framework in which to place the objects — Modernist or Medieval, machine or musical instrument, tool or torso — but the readings remain beyond resolution, and the best we can come up with is that they are between categories. Fane is aware of this, and remarks that "many of Taccola's drawings seem impossible to understand, and that is a connection that I feel with my work — I never quite find the reading for them, nor do I really want to." There are other long-standing formal influences at work here — African, Romanesque, and especially folk art, which Fane appreciates "for its freedom and informality, and the fact that it is so persuasive without necessarily being so well made." Fane's discovery of Taccola's drawings has allowed him to understand and synthesize these disparate influences and integrate them into his work in a wholly new and convincing way.

What is it that Fane found so compelling in the work of Taccola? There is no simple answer to this question. The nature of inspiration is perhaps the most difficult to account for in the study of art. The best one can hope to do is make a few educated guesses. Fane admits that he has "a missionary sense about this man, for reasons I can't begin to explain." Some helpful clues to the attraction are contained in Fane's own writings on Taccola For example, he discusses his admiration for Taccola's drawings by referring to "their animated theatricality, their creation of a fantasy world in which mechanical inventions become protagonists in a massive sort of theatre," and further states, "Taccola's method of representation falls between accepted categories, and is idiosyncratic and original," and finally, "his drawings have such authority that they create their own convincing worlds of reality." I think we can say that the qualities Fane describes as so endearing in Taccola's work are qualities that apply equally well to his own work and indicate that a certain degree of artistic transference has taken place. Fane is aware of the process by which an artist absorbs a source of inspiration so thoroughly that the influence is only discovered in retrospect as a kind of confirmation of his own ideas. In this regard, Fane cites a statement from an interview with the author Joyce Cary (1888-1957) about the main character in Cary's novel *The Horse's Mouth:* "When someone asked him once if the hero, Gulley Jimson, was a real artist that he knew or did he invent him, Cary said 'Yes, he was a real artist but I didn't meet him until after the novel was written.'"

For most of his career, Fane has been

attracted by art and visual culture that have not been common as a source of inspiration for much of contemporary art. As we have seen, tools have been very important to him, especially the antique hand tools he collects that are odd or surprising in some way and have affinities with some of his own formal ideas. Other sources have been medieval or Renaissance artists who are obscure even to specialists in the field: artists such as Tino di Camaino (1280-1377), Agostino di Duccio, and of course Taccola. These artists straddle the accepted categories of medieval and Renaissance engineer and scientist, artist, and inventor, and they are unappreciated for no other reason than that they are not easily placed into the conventional narratives of art history.

Fane's borrowings from these artists are never overt copies of their work but are similar to his tool collections — they are sources of abstraction and confirm the correctness of his own formal intuition. Fane is unusually respectful and open about his sources, never seeming to want to discount or erase the past. In the case of Taccola, Fane, through his writings on the artist, seems more motivated by a desire to upgrade the reputation of an artist who has been classified improperly than to call attention to himself (although by reclassifying Taccola he is also in effect reclassifying himself as an artist). Fane could have just as easily chosen to hide his sources (no one would ever have known), but he chose not to. His enthusiasm for the artist is infectious, but underlying it is a need to recuperate some vital aspect from the past and give it a new and better life, and in so doing, to claim a living portion of that past for himself. There is a thoughtful and rare suspension of the egocentric in much of Fane's work that belies the popular image of an artist as an *enfant terrible*, given to irrational thoughts, moods, and gestures. Fane offers us an alternative model: an artist secure in his sense of self and skills, engaged in an extended creative dialogue with the traditional and the modern, and who does not feel it necessary to reject either.

The tension between tradition and modernity has haunted Modern art since its inception, and each generation of artists has to position itself in relation to this issue, as the pendulum swings between the two poles. As we have seen, it was the tradition of the artist-engineer that made such an impact on Fane. A tradition is by definition something one needs to inherit — an artist cannot invent it. One recalls Mercedes Matter's warning that, once separated from the tradition of the studio, art education threatens to devolve into an exercise of meaningless self-deception. And this has become the predicament that artists have faced since the 1960s, its legacy being the Postmodern "tradition-of-no-tradition." Anything goes, and nothing seems to satisfy for more than a season or two. However, Fane's training was different — he *had* inherited a tradition, a very potent one centered on drawing and the study of anatomy, but it lacked a correspondingly convincing aesthetic vision. One might guess that what was so appealing about his discovery of the artist-engineer tradition was that it offered him a bridge between his own internal divisions, giving him access to a more comprehensive vision of life and art. Taccola's example, so vividly expressed in his drawings, offers us evidence that there did exist a time and place where art and science were not the mutually exclusive categories they are today, and Fane's creative response to Taccola's work provides us a view of an imaginative world in which that dream is still alive.

CODA: FANE'S DREAM OF TACCOLA

A sculpture from 1997, *Taccola's Dream* (cat. no. 17, page 49), is a good example of the fantasy world that Fane has created and inhabited with the mechanical inventions that make up his Taccola series. The work is a long floor-hugging wooden "device" of some sort that is supported on three legs, two of which are angled outward to give the impression of an animal in a guarding position. The horizontal transverse element has the abstracted form of a torso or tuning fork that has been stretched lengthwise. This beautifully attenuated shape has a channel-like division running along its length, terminating at what would appear to be the business-end of the sculpture, and it is rich with associations. One is reminded of Brancusi's slender

abstractions as well as the Cubists' love for conflating female contours with the shapes of violins or guitars. Its rough, textured surface and simple but efficient-looking geometry recall the work of Dogon carvers. The reverie of human form is interrupted by the overriding impression that the object serves a utilitarian function. A long and sturdy-looking shaft, parallel to the horizontal plane, reinforces the sense that the object may be a machine of some kind: a machine with human attributes, made by a highly skilled artisan — something we might come across in a museum of technology in an alternative, more humanistically evolved universe than our own.[14]

Artists of all eras have been fascinated by the beauty and power of machines. On a purely practical level, this is because they need to make things, and machines and tools enable them to do so efficiently by extending the power of the hand. As a theme in art, the merging of the qualities of the mechanical and the human has a very long history that runs from seventeenth-century *automata* to the cyborgs of today. As we have seen, Fane has spent the better part of his career studying the anatomy of men and machines, and the ease with which he traverses these categories is reflected in his work. In our postindustrial world, the mechanical has more often played a sinister role, contributing to our diminished sense of communal relationship — turning us into a society of competing individuals. The Faustian bargain between science and industry so deeply imbedded in the fabric of our corporate economic system has rendered us indifferent to the natural world around us. We would like to act and feel as humans, but more often we behave like machines.

When we consider Fane's work of the last ten years, we are confronted with a sensibility that appreciates the mechanical in a disarmingly optimistic way. Fane's humanized machines call to us from another world — a preindustrial world at the dawn of the Renaissance — that was also the center of the canon of Western art and civilization. It was a world where man was the measure of all things. Fane's sculptures evoke a culture that values equally the productions of the hand, eye, and mind — a place and time where art, science, and industry co-exist in a fragile but harmonious balance of power. These values have long been forgotten or, as Fane might characterize it, misplaced, following the collapse of the coherent world-view of the Renaissance and the ascendancy of the modern industrial state. In the artist's rediscovery of the humanism of Taccola's artist-engineer tradition, we are gently encouraged to follow Fane's example and reevaluate our fundamental vision of the world. His "machines of the mind" beckon us to rise to a higher and more noble vision of ourselves — a preexisting, one hesitates to say, ready-made vision that, with a few artful tailorings, might enhance our existence and enrich the meaning of our lives. That Fane manages this impressive feat through the persuasive creations of his intelligent hands must be considered something of a modernist miracle.

BILL BARRETTE

ENDNOTES

1. *Arts Magazine,* September 1963.

2. *Marcel Duchamp* (New York: Museum of Modern Art, 1973).

3. As for Fane and Demetrios, they had considerable differences in background and temperament, but in spite of that, their close relationship would prove to be an enduring one. One thus has to assume that it satisfied some essential need for each. Demetrios felt a paternal and vicarious pride in his talented student even after Fane decided to go his own way and "become a Modernist," and years later, Fane would honor his teacher by naming his son after him. They remained close until Demetrios's death in 1974, with Fane frequently spending summers working in Gloucester, where interaction between the two artists was familial rather than artistic.

4. Clement Greenberg, "Modernist Painting," radio broadcast, Lecture 14 in *The Voice of America Forum Lectures: The Visual Arts* of 1961. Later published by the United States Information Agency (Washington, DC, 1965).

5. Anne Rorimer, *New Art in the 60s and 70s: Redefining Reality* (London: Thames and Hudson, 2001).

6. The legacy of this cool, hands-off attitude toward the creation of sculpture is evident today, although not applied with the same ideological rigor of Sol LeWitt or Donald Judd. Instead, we observe the phenomenon of the young "shooting-star" artist, catapulted to the stage of the international circuit, turning to ever more elaborate and expensive stratagems of fabrication to maintain a competitive edge in the marketplace. Attend the Whitney Biennial, Venice Biennale, or even the latest oversized Chelsea galleries, and one often gets the impression of witnessing a Disneyesque battle-of-the-fabricators, with size, special effects, and the display of the power of the artist's patrons being the most notable aesthetic consideration.

7. Robert Hughes, "The Aesthete as Popeye," *Time,* August 13, 2001.

8. This is not an isolated example of the acknowledgment of the importance of an older artist: Fane described a steel work from 1976, called *Ladish 6,* as "an homage to Brancusi and a Constructivist answer to his *A Bird in Flight.*"

9. The fragmentary nature of Fane's work, as well as the combination of figurative and landscape elements, recalls the work of the French sculptor Jean Ipousteguy, who showed briefly in New York in the 1970s. There is an affinity at this time to the forged sculptures of the German sculptor Rudolf Hoflehner, whose work also has an erotic/abstract quality.

10. James L. Flint, *The Automobile Age* (Cambridge, MA: MIT Press, 1988).

11. *David Smith in Italy* (Milan: Edizioni Charta, 1994).

12. In a curious coincidence, Duchamp's ready-mades and Ford's assembly line were to make their first appearances within a year of each other, 1913 and 1914.

13. Lawrence Fane, "The Invented World of Mariano Taccola: Re-visiting a Once Famous Artist-Engineer of 15th Century Italy," in *Leonardo: Journal of the International Society for the Arts, Sciences and Technology* (MIT Press), forthcoming.

14. The inspiration for the piece is essentially Taccola's engineering drawings of devices to channel the flow of water. Strangely, when asked about this piece, Fane told the story of having gone to the Tilman Riemenschneider exhibition at the Metropolitan Museum of Art after his piece was finished. Riemenschneider (circa 1460-1531), a Late Gothic sculptor, was among the greatest wood carvers of his time, and Fane was familiar with Riemenschneider's work but was astonished when he saw the sculptor's workbench included in the exhibition. He realized that it was exactly the same size as his recently finished piece, had similar legs, and a turning device — it was in fact a machine for making sculptures, an association that links it nicely with Fane's sculptures. The coincidence between the two objects, of course, pleased him, and was another in a long line of confirmations that his work is part of a family of three-dimensional idea-forms that go back centuries and know no temporal, national, or geographic boundaries.

Pylon

1991

welded steel, polychromed, 37 x 31 x 40 inches

Marsh Art Gallery, University of Richmond Museums,

Gift of Bernard and Ninon Chaet

(cat. no. 3)

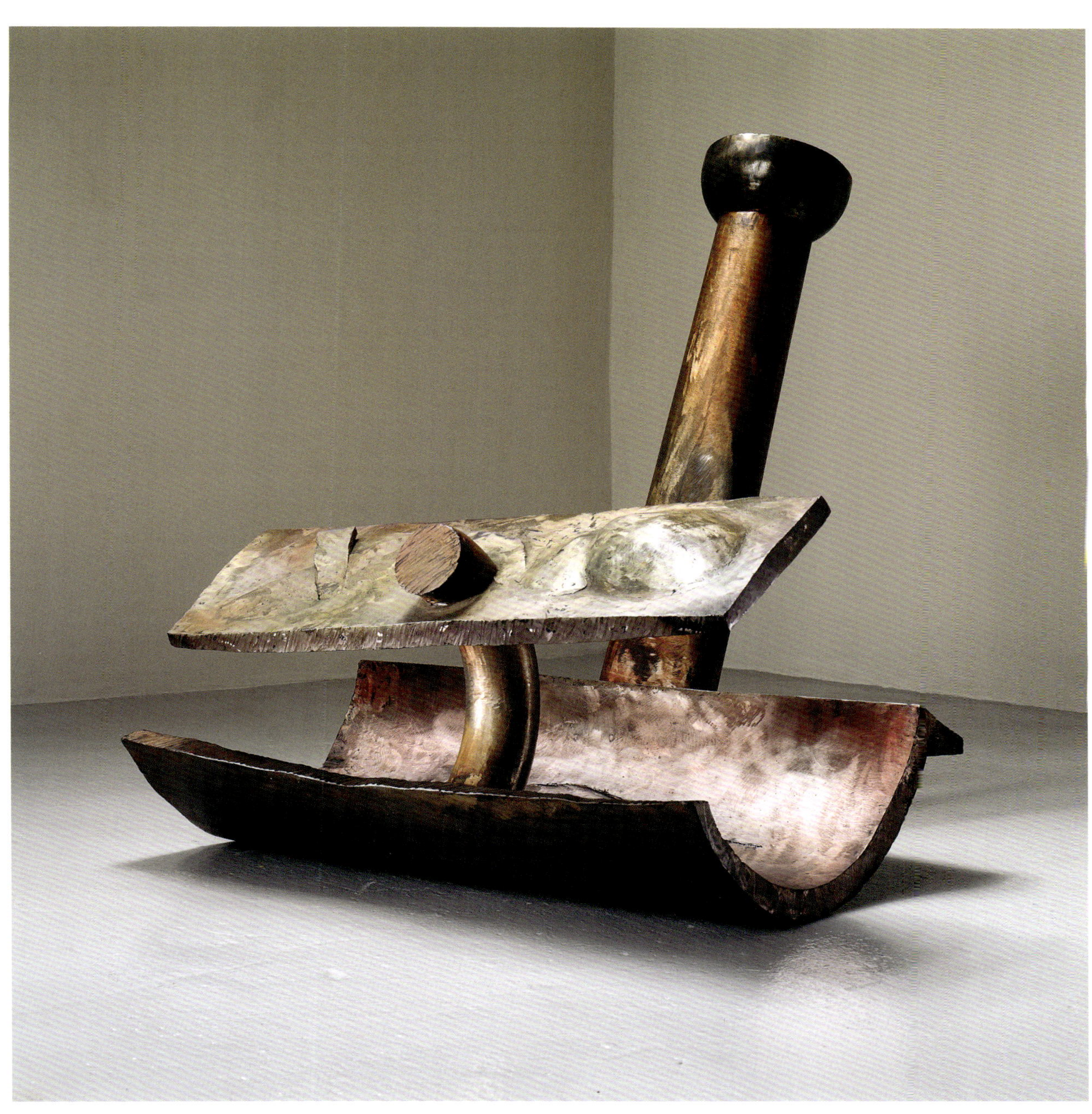

Omphalos

1991-92

welded steel, 79 x 72 x 122 inches

Collection of the artist

(cat. no. 5)

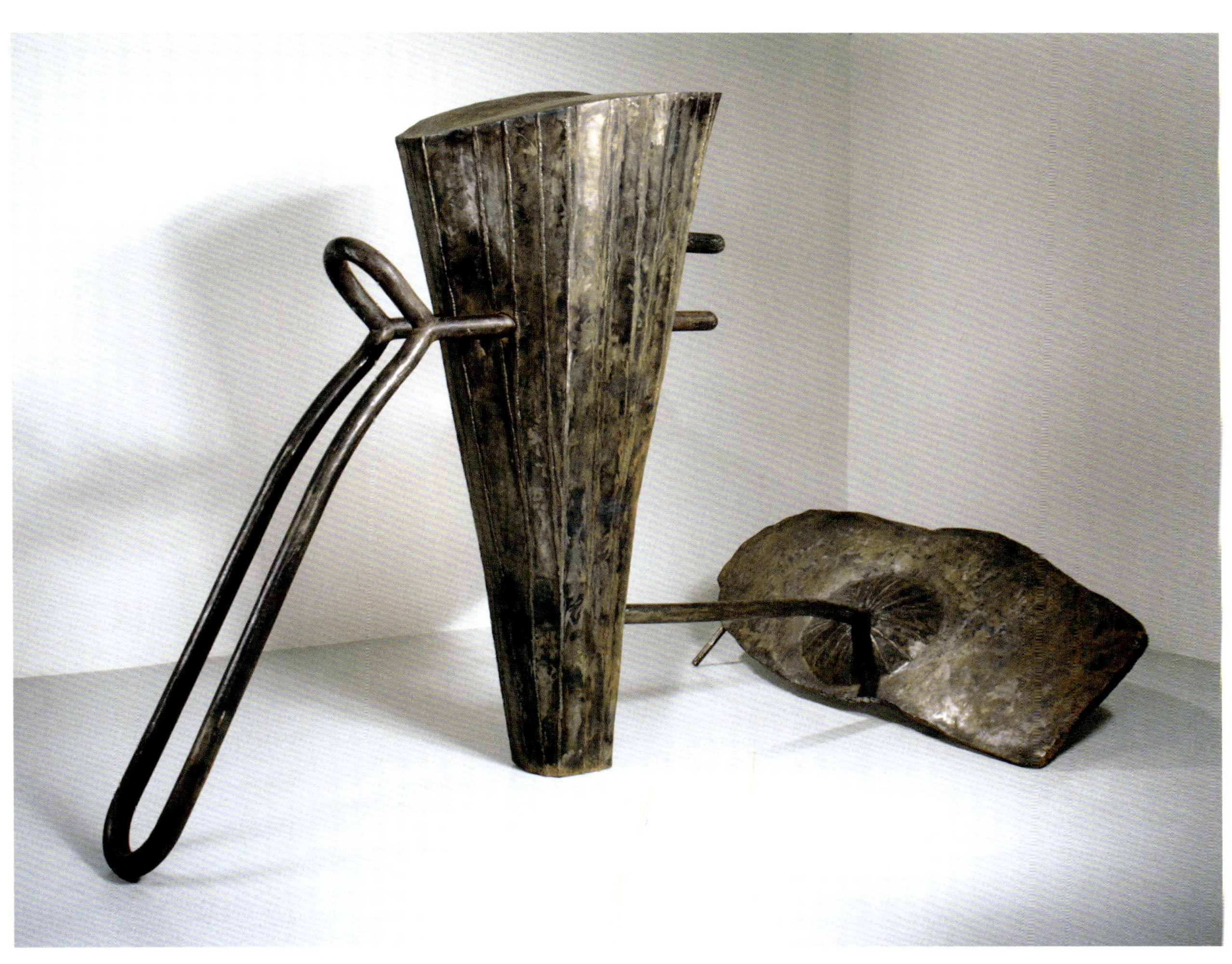

Sanctus

1994

wood, polychromed, 58 x 35 x 35 inches

Collection of Anthea Fane

(cat. no. 9)

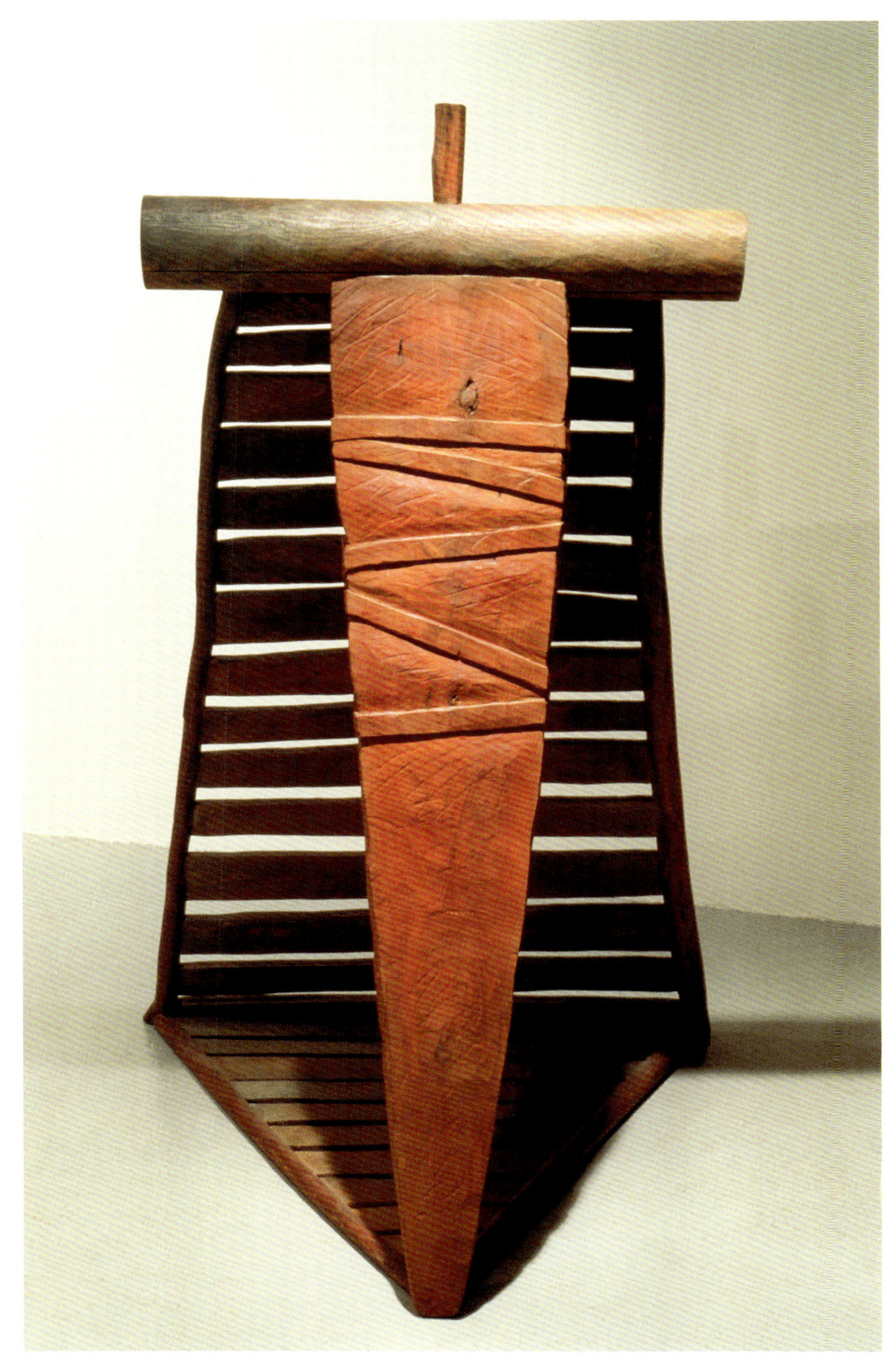

Mound

1994

wood, polychromed, 17 x 13 x 16 inches

Collection of the artist

(cat. no. 10)

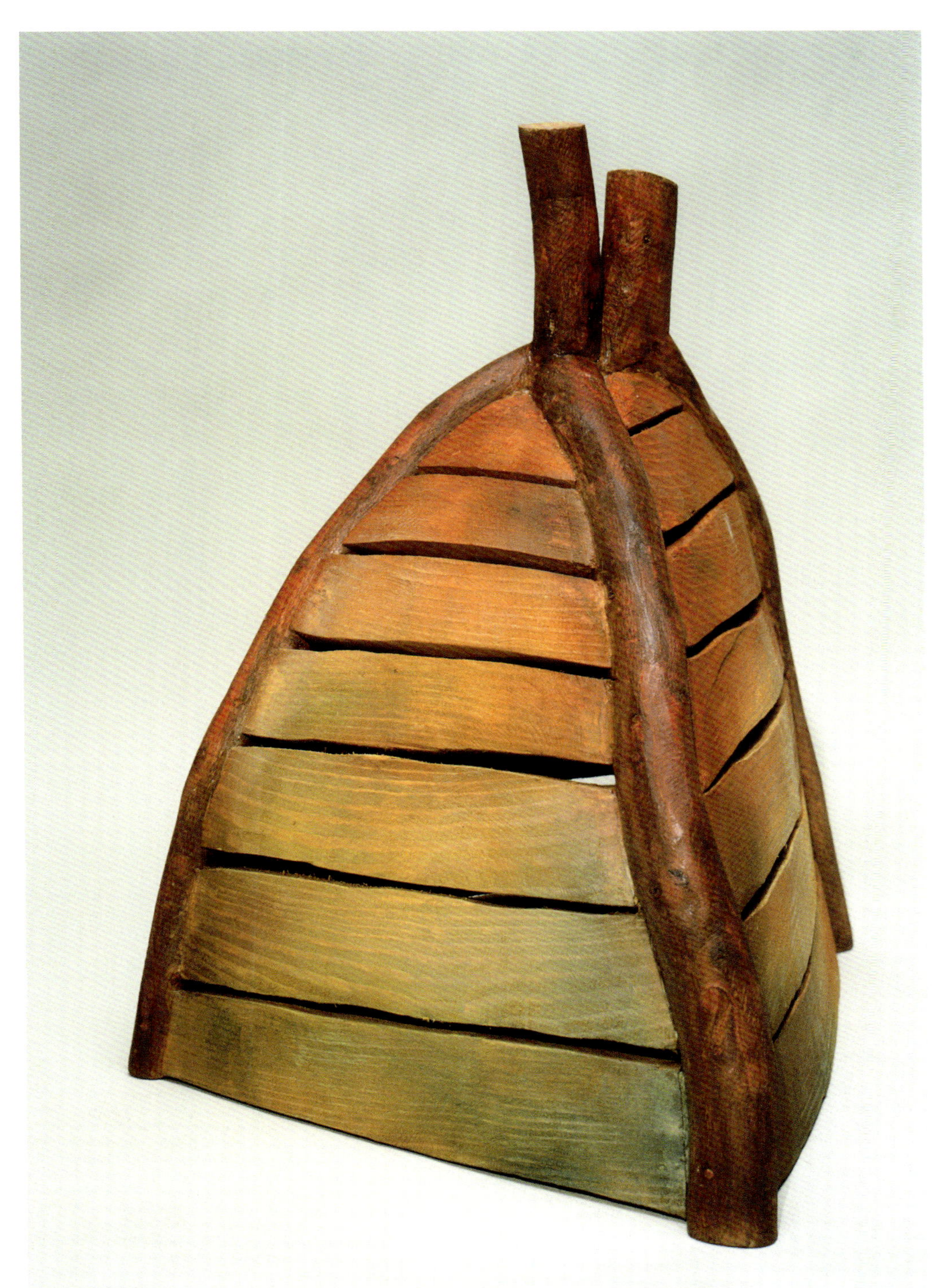

Center 1

1994

wood, 21 x 52 x 56 inches

Collection of Dimitri Fane

(cat. no. 12)

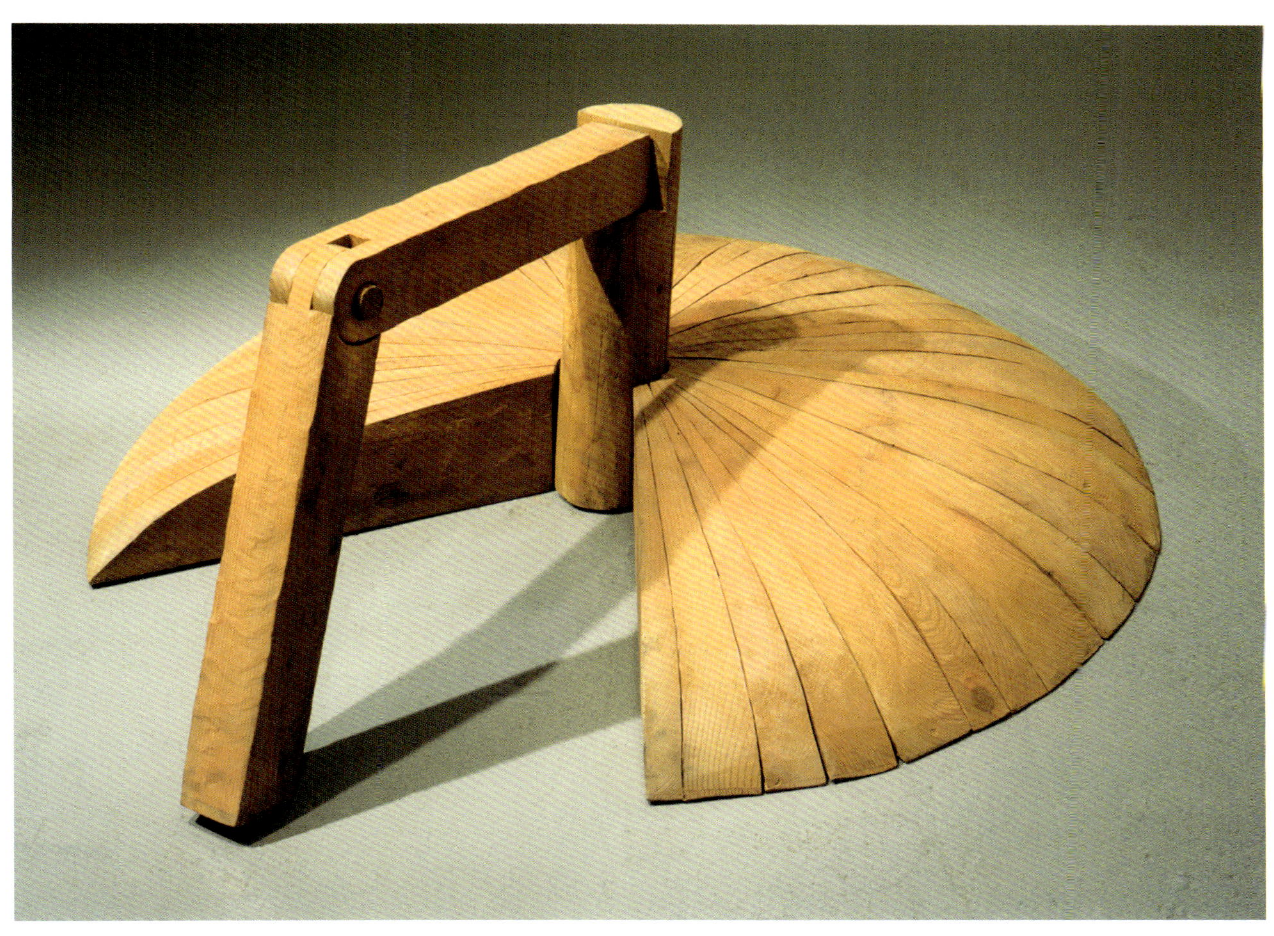

Chamber

1996

wood, polychromed, 32 x 12 x 28 inches

Lent courtesy of Kouros Gallery, New York

(cat. no. 13)

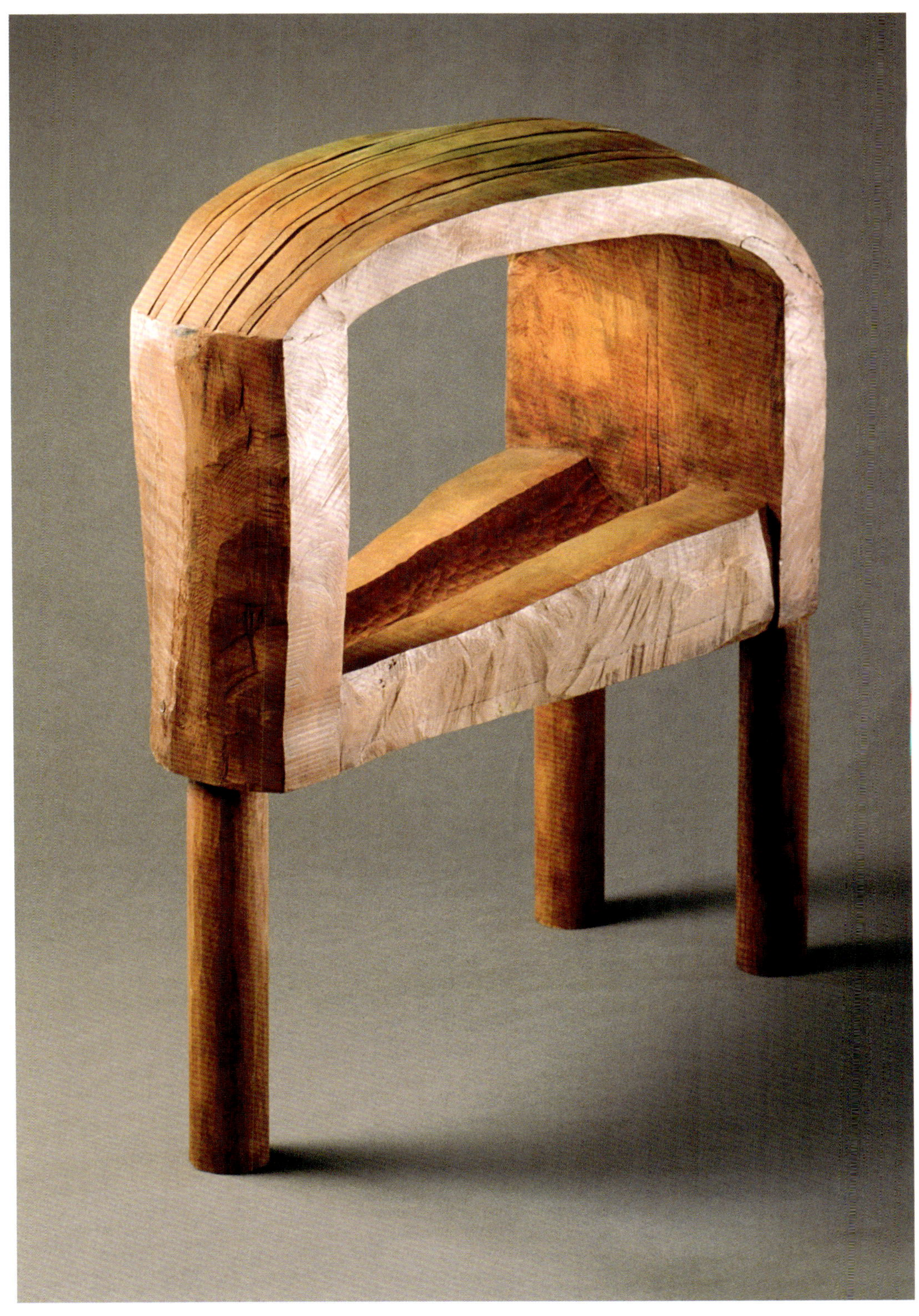

Mantle

1996-97

wood, 25 x 38 x 28 inches

Lent courtesy of Kouros Gallery, New York

(cat. no. 15)

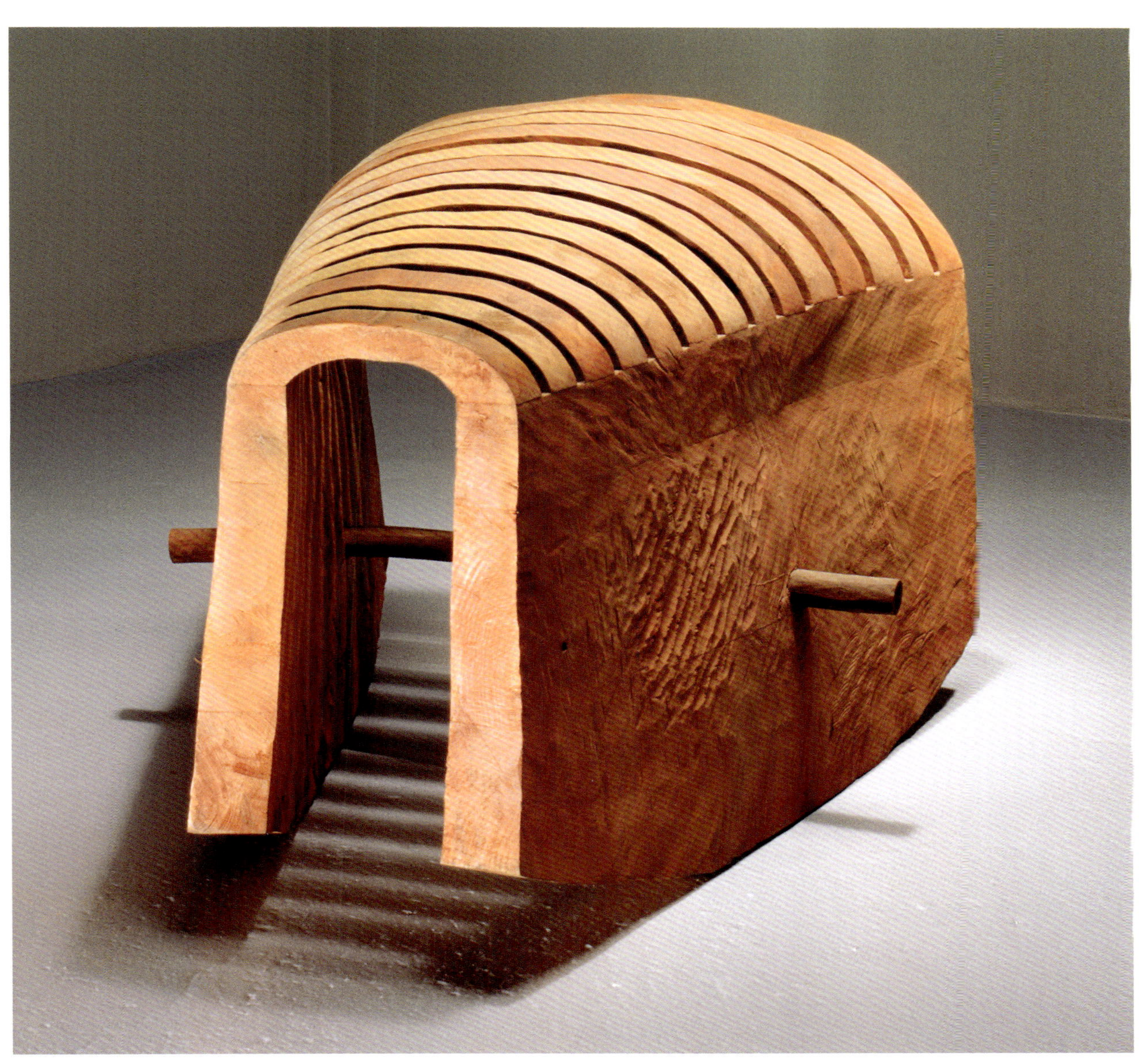

Taccola's Dream

1997

wood, 41 x 84 x 31 inches

Lent courtesy of Kouros Gallery, New York

(cat. no. 17)

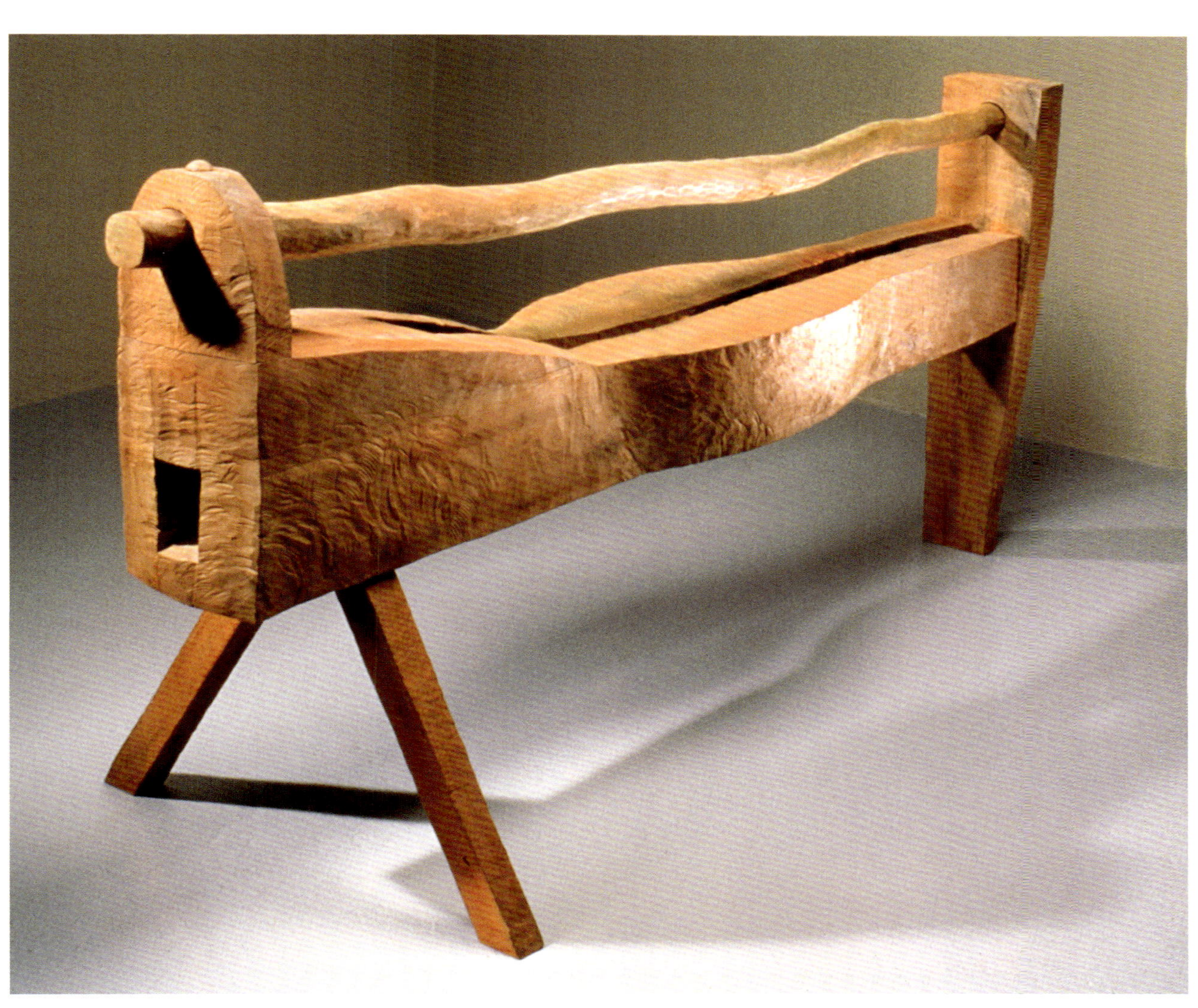

Barrel

1997-98

wood and steel, 27 x 24 x 8 inches

Lent courtesy of Kouros Gallery, New York

(cat. no. 19)

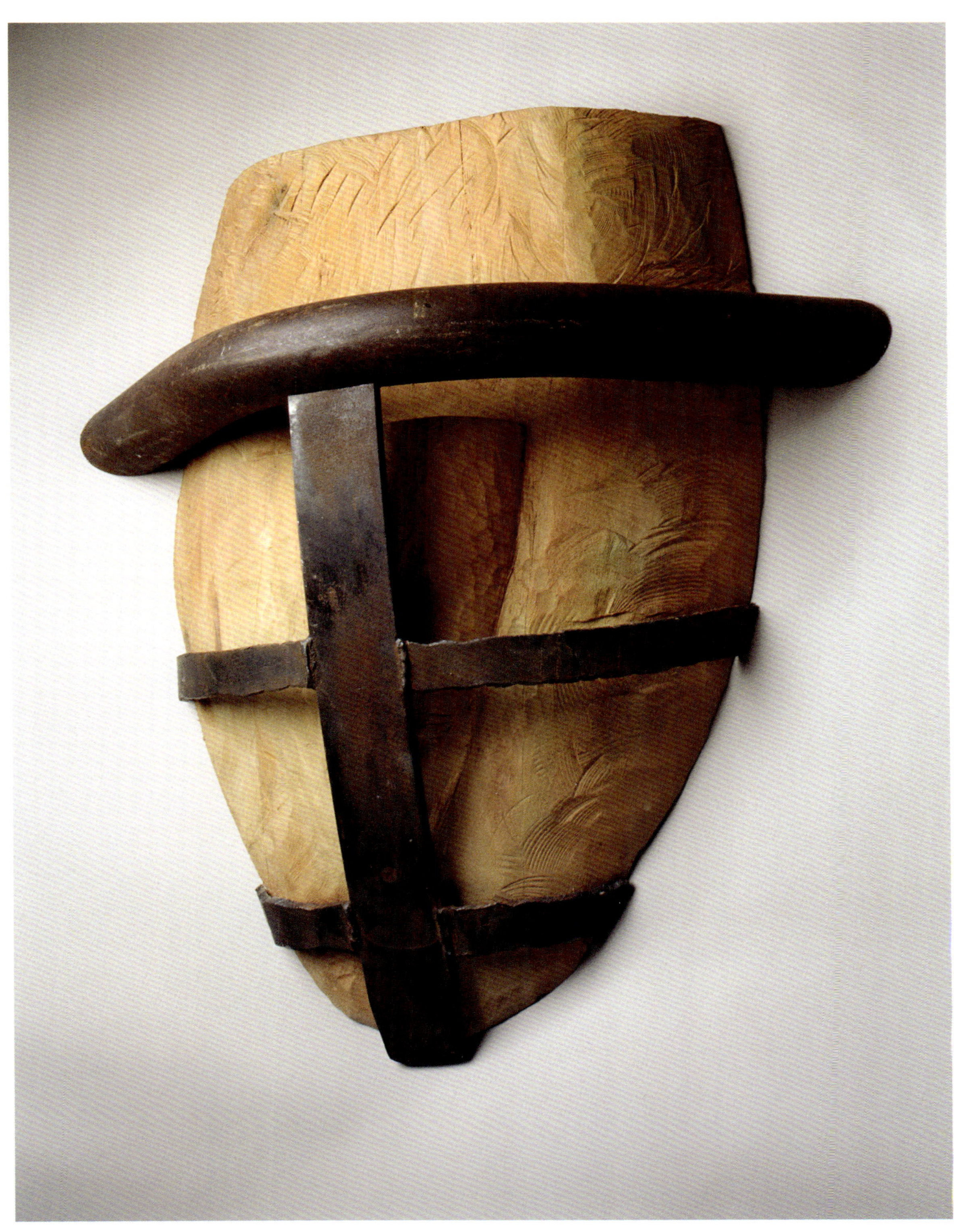

Pendant

1998

wood and steel, 27 x 8 x 11 inches

Lent courtesy of Kouros Gallery, New York

(cat. no. 20)

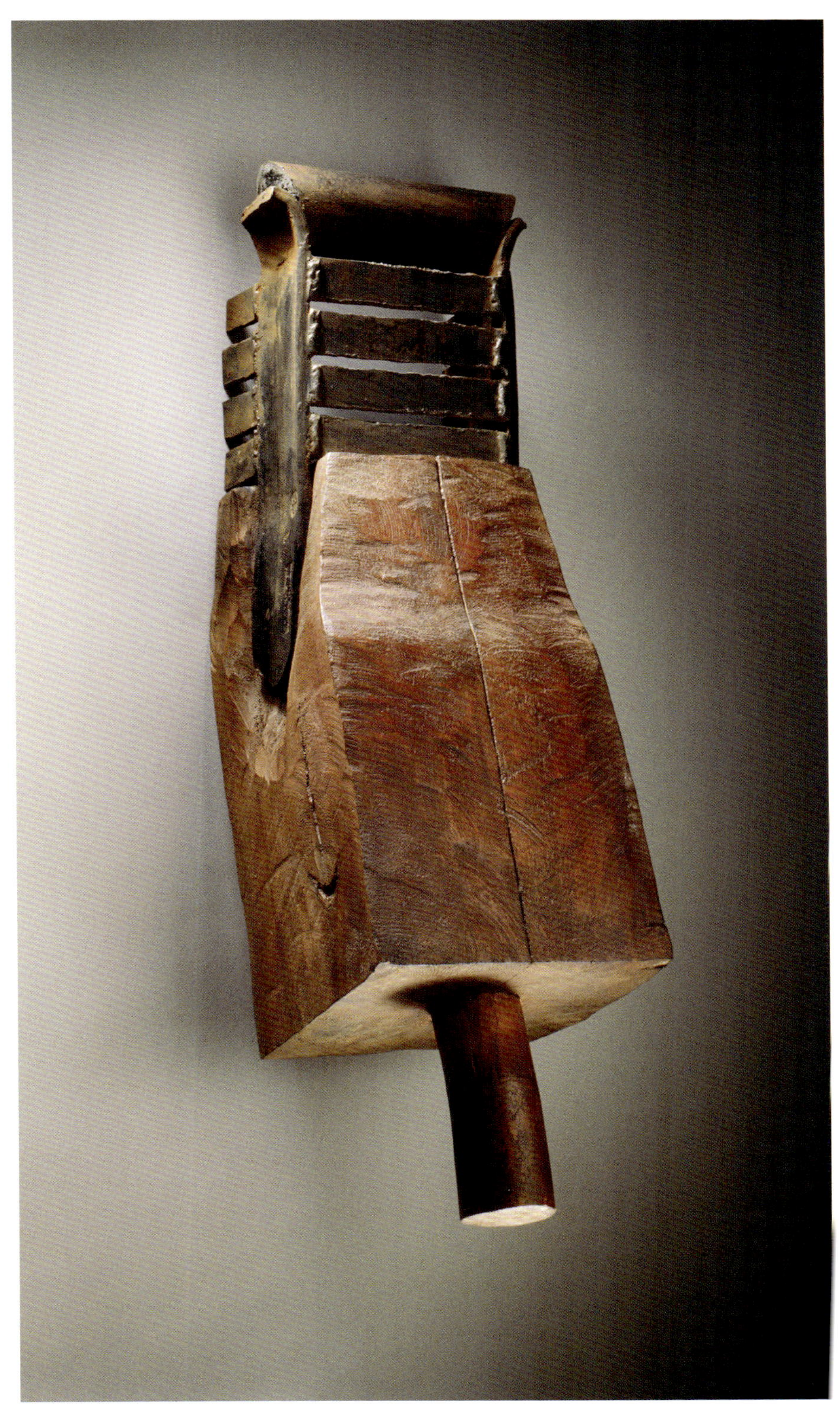

Mill Piece

1998

wood, polychromed, 73 x 42 x 60 inches

Lent courtesy of Kouros Gallery, New York

(cat. no. 21)

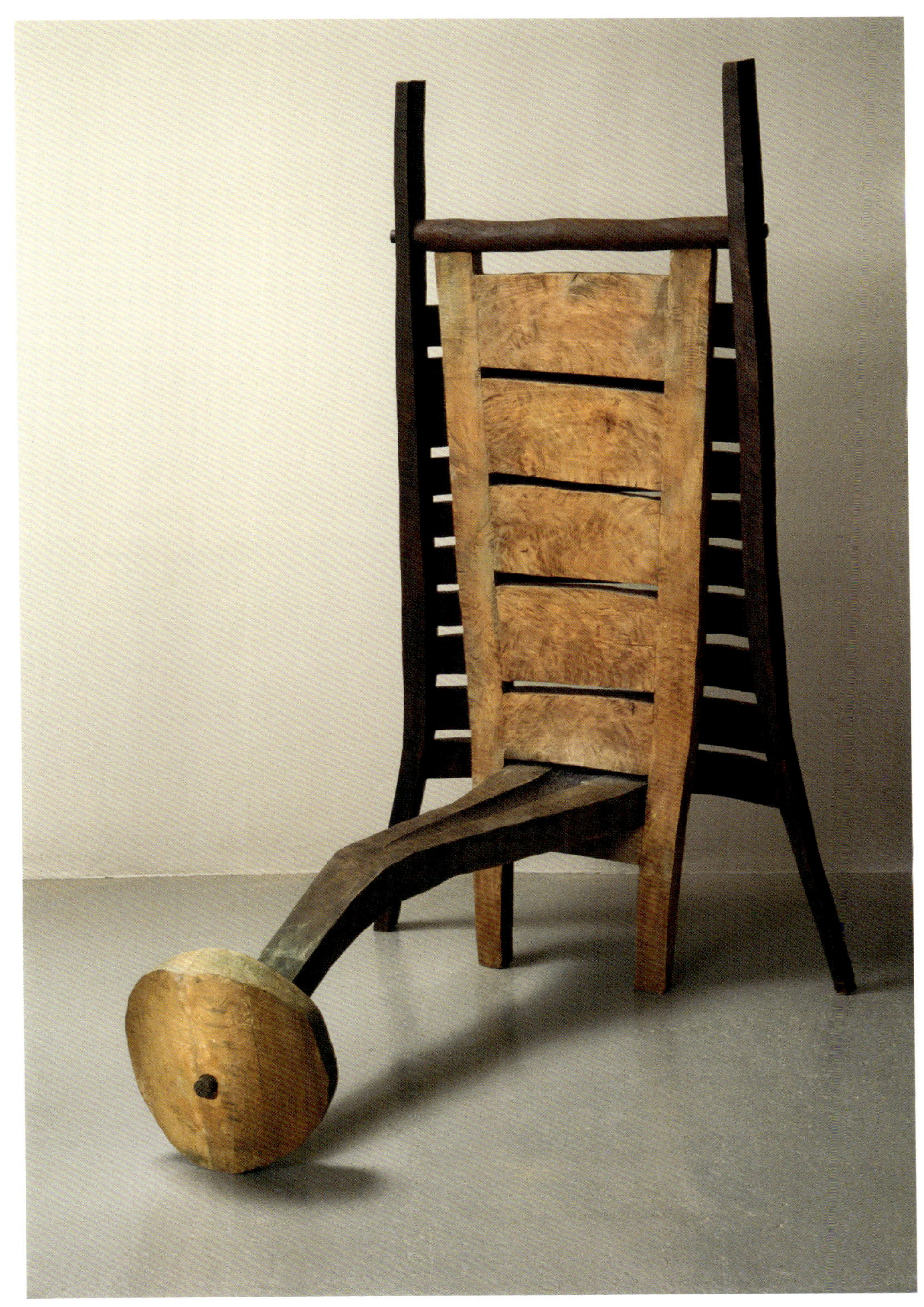

Cask

1999

concrete and wood, 46 x 18 x 28 inches

Collection of the artist

(cat. no. 22)

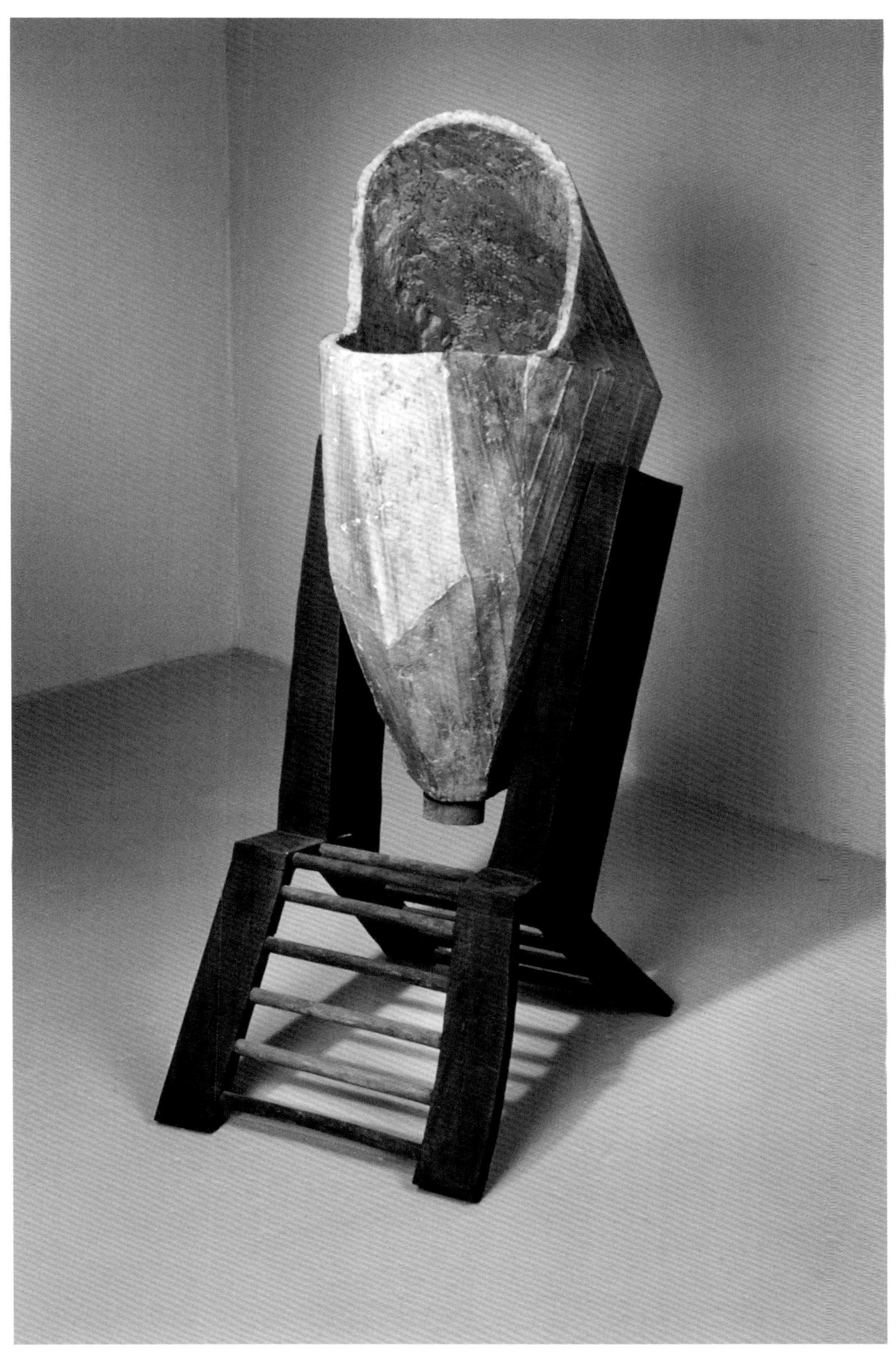

Table

1999-2000

wood, stains, 39 x 9 x 36 inches

Collection of the artist

(cat. no. 23)

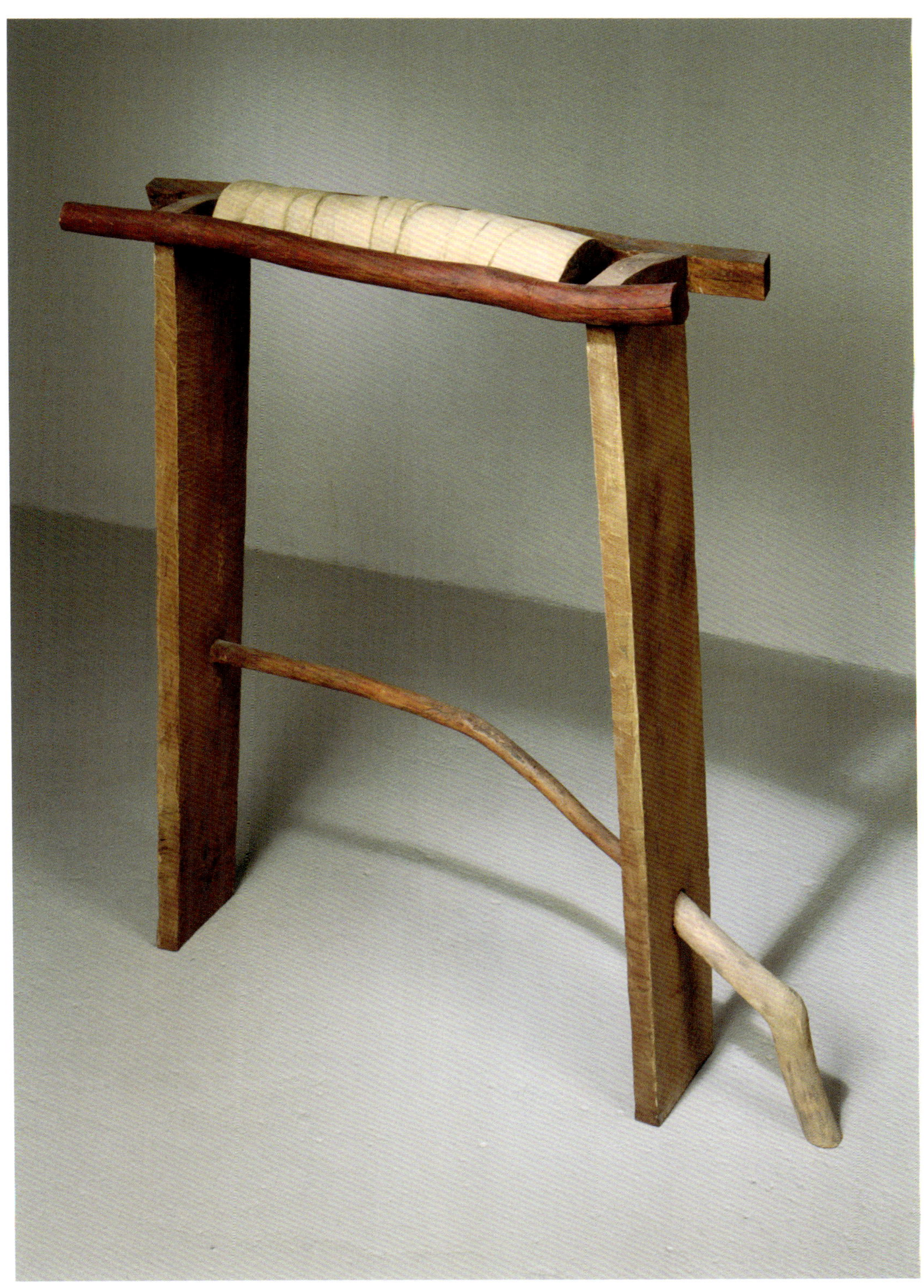

Roller

1999-2000

wood, 33 x 18 x 39 inches

Collection of the artist

(cat. no. 24)

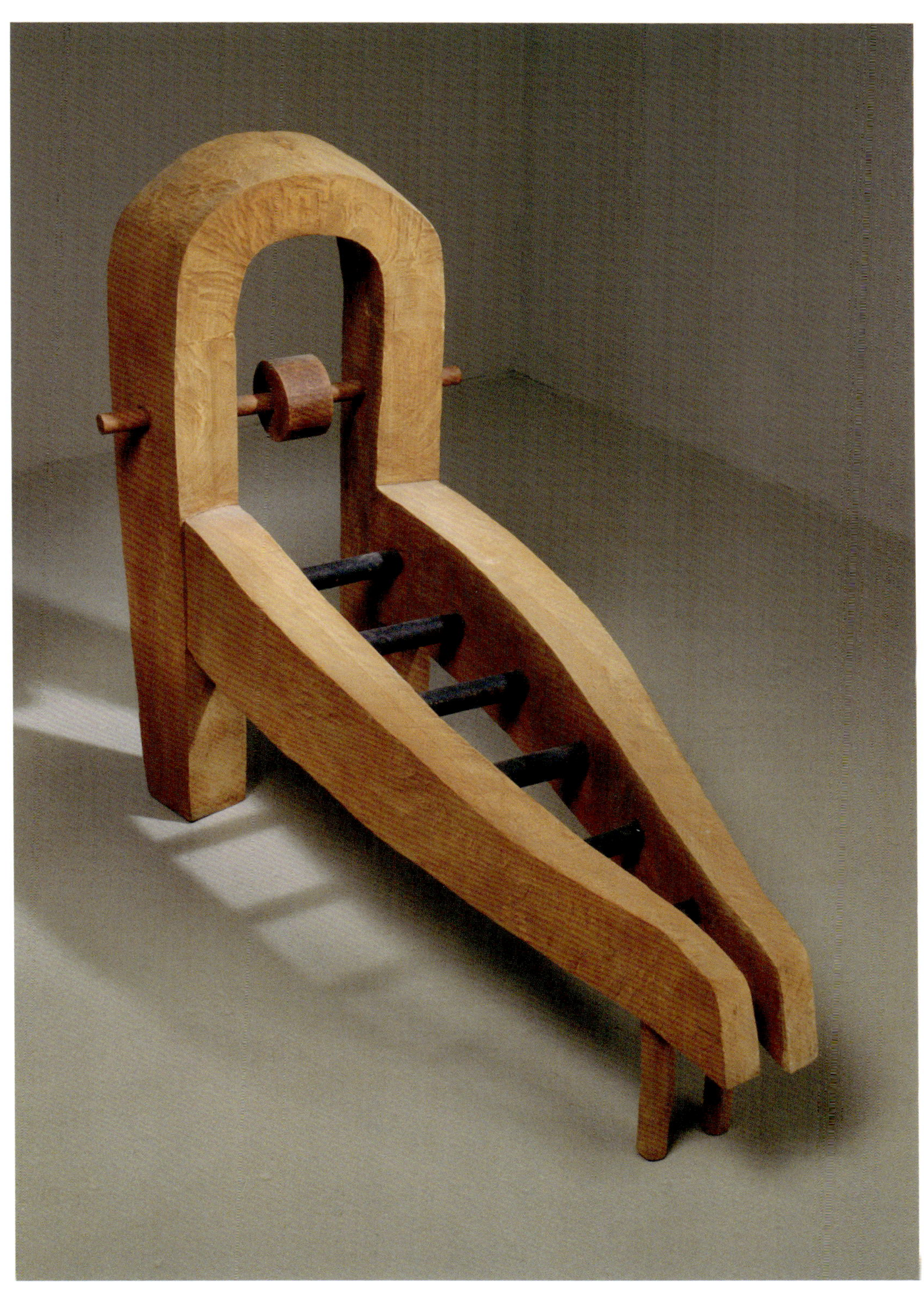

Source

2000

concrete and wood, 54 x 22 x 26 inches

Collection of the artist

(cat. no. 25)

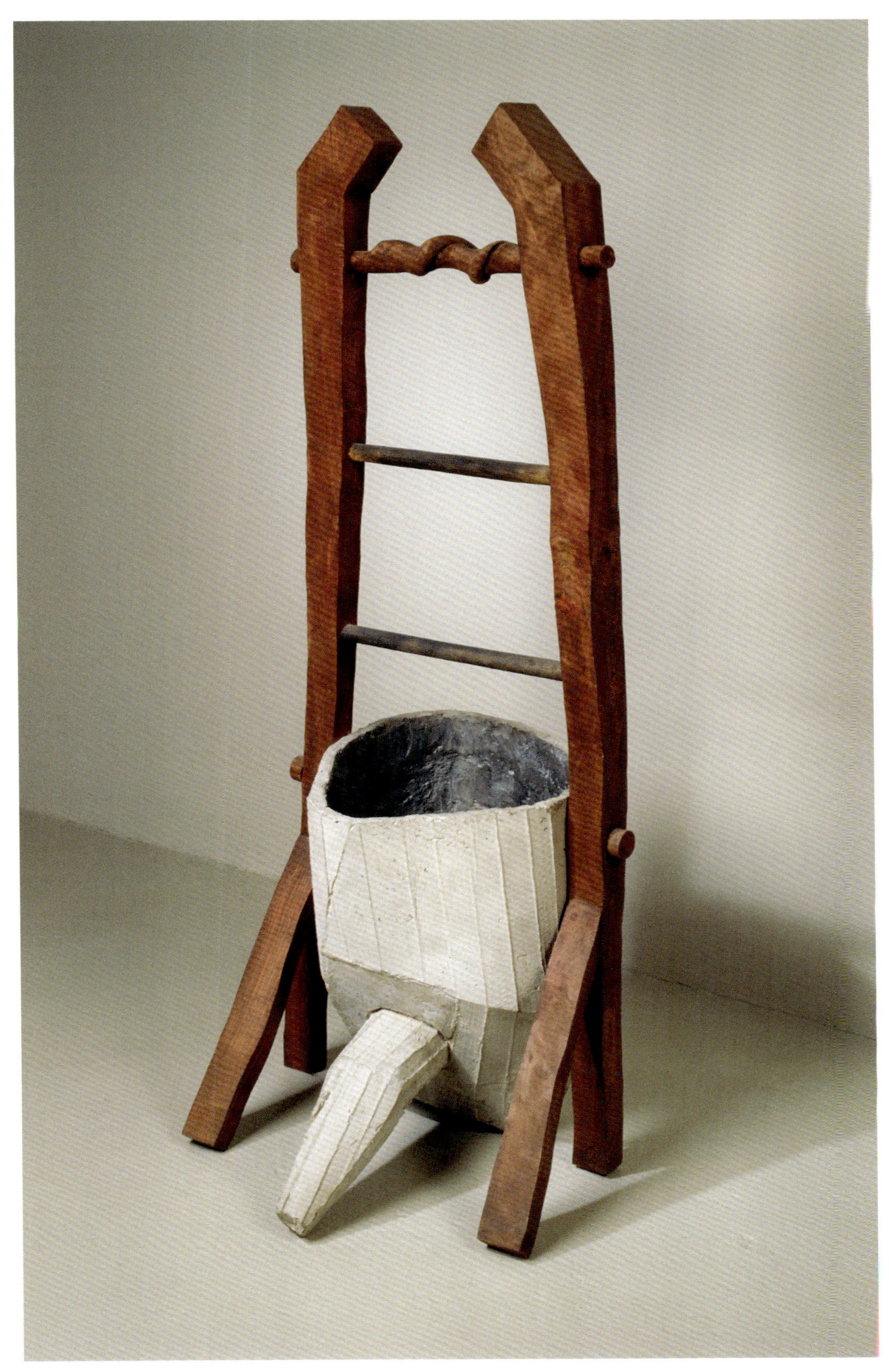

Mount

2001

concrete, stains, 15 x 12 x 17 inches

Collection of the artist

(cat. no. 28)

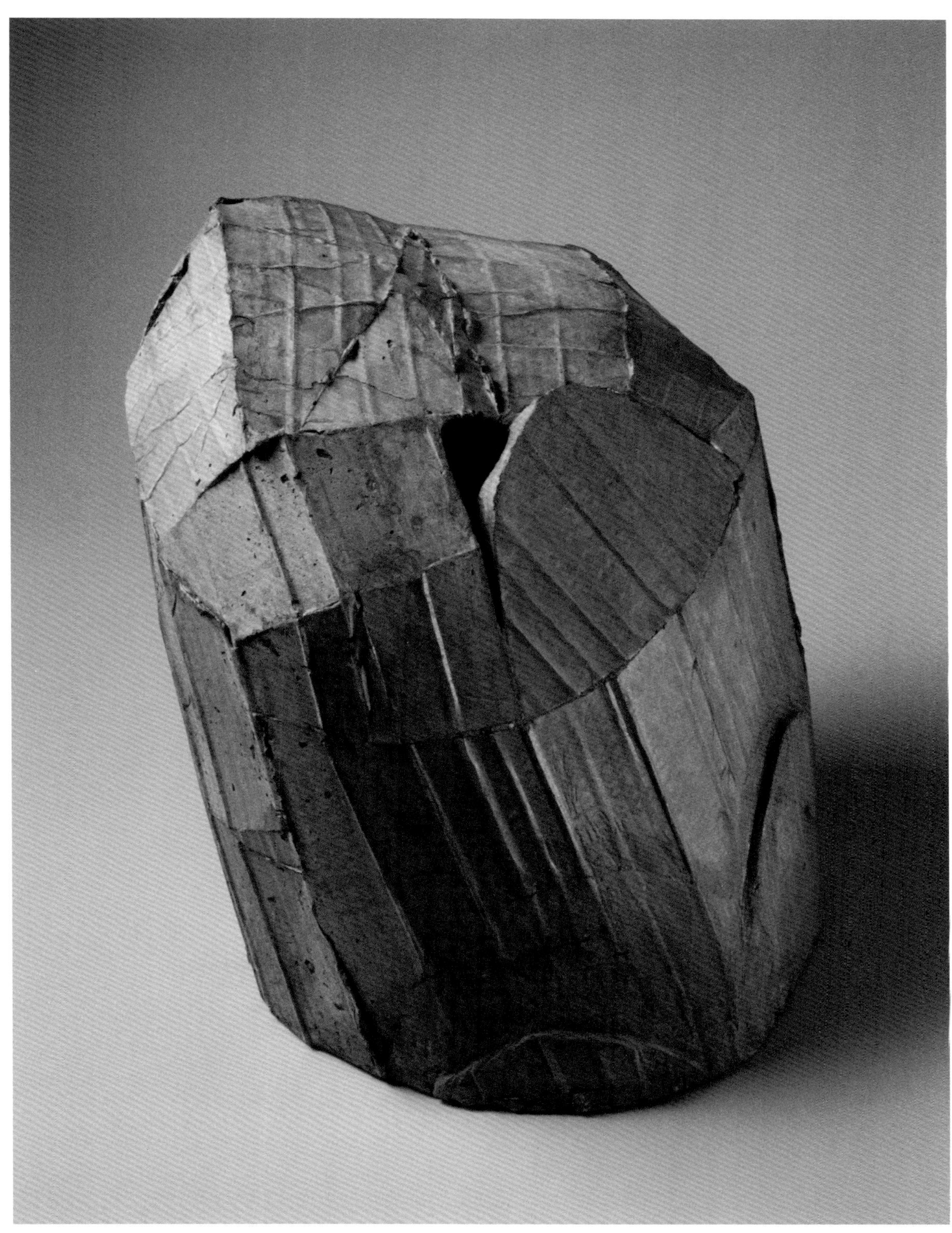

Filter

2001

concrete and steel, stains, 20 x 17 x 10 inches

Collection of the artist

(cat. no. 29)

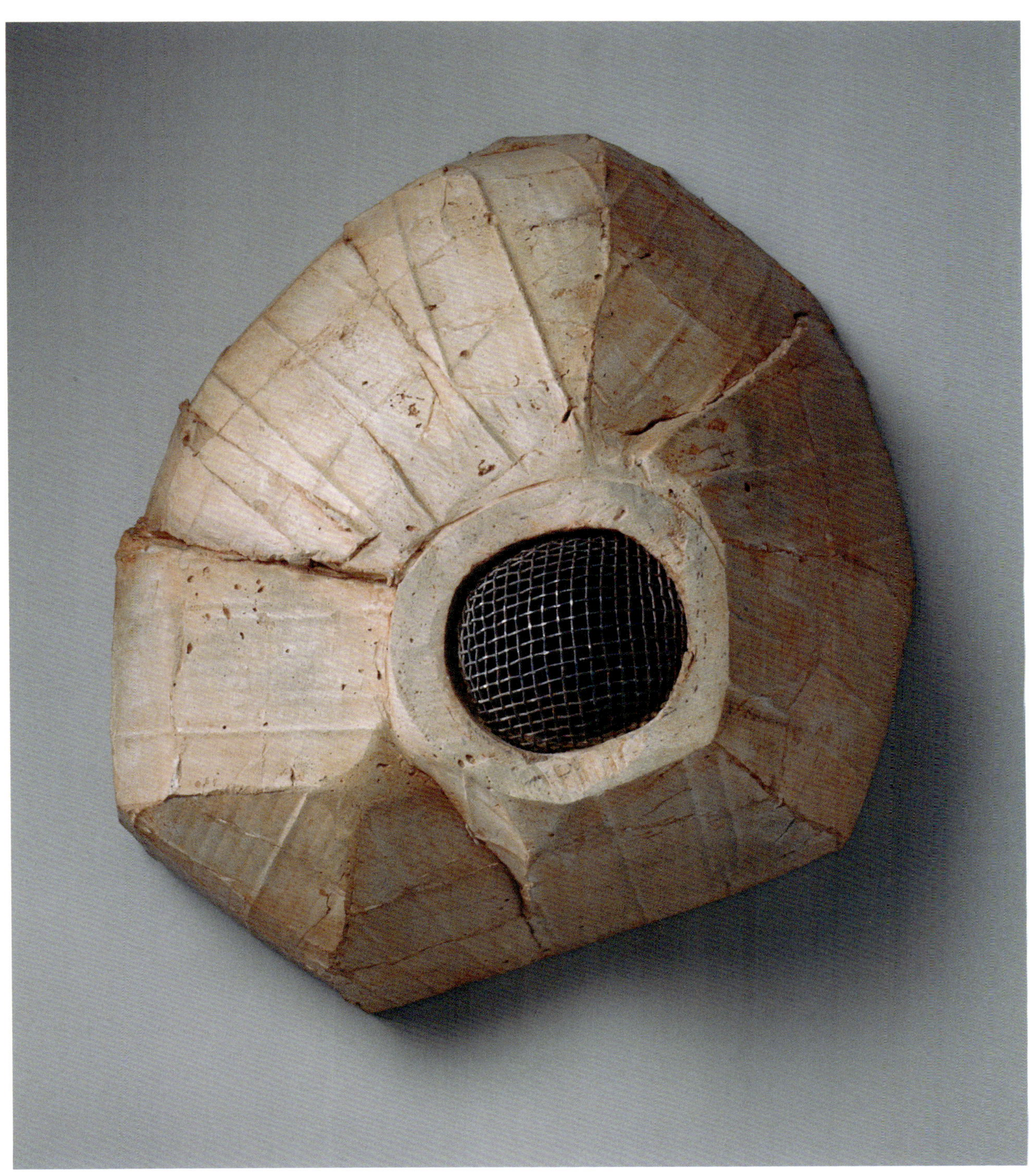

Born 1933 in Kansas City, Missouri.
Resides New York.

Education

1957-1960
Student and assistant to George Demetrios, Boston, MA.
1955-1956
School of the Museum of Fine Arts, Boston, MA.
1952-1955
B.A., Harvard University, Cambridge, MA.

Teaching Positions

1966-1998
Queens College, City University of New York.
1963-1966
Rhode Island School of Design, Providence, RI.

Selected Awards

1997
New York Foundation for the Arts, Artist's Fellowship.
1994, 1986
Research Foundation, City University of New York.
1984, 1973
Ingram Merrill Foundation Fellowship
1962, 1961, 1960
Rome Prize, American Academy in Rome.

Selected Individual Exhibitions

2002
Machines of the Mind: Sculpture by Lawrence Fane, Marsh Art Gallery, University of Richmond Museums, VA, and Muscarelle Museum of Art, The College of William and Mary, Williamsburg, VA (catalogue).
2000
Chamot Gallery, Jersey City, NJ.
1999
Kouros Gallery, NY (catalogue).
1996
Jaffe-Friede & Straus Galleries, Dartmouth College, Hanover, NH.
Ben Shahn Galleries, William Paterson University of New Jersey, Wayne.
1995
Bill Bace Gallery, NY.
1993
Recent Sculpture, Brooks Hall Gallery, School of Design, State University of North Carolina, Raleigh, traveled to Bill Bace Gallery, NY (catalogue).
1991
Bill Bace Gallery, NY.
1985
Marilyn Pearl Galley, NY.
1983
Washington Art Association, Washington, CT.
1982
Marilyn Pearl Galley, NY.

1980
Stones of Gloucester, Spazio Oolp, Turin, Italy.
1978
Marilyn Pearl Gallery, NY.
1977
Bard College, Annandale-on-Hudson, NY.
Duke University, Durham, NC.
1976
Marilyn Pearl Galley, NY.
1969
Zabriskie Gallery, NY.

Selected Group Exhibitions

2000
Selections from the Permanent Collection, Marsh Art Gallery, University of Richmond Museums, VA.
Annual Invitational Exhibition, American Academy of Arts and Letters, NY.
1999
Artists Who Lived in Gloucester, Cape Ann Historical Museum, Gloucester, MA.
1998
Bridging: Man and Nature, Williamsburg Art and Historical Center, Brooklyn, NY.
1997
Recent Acquisitions, Brooklyn Museum of Art, NY.
Sit on This: The Chair as Art, The Society of the Four Arts, Palm Beach, FL.

1996
Annual Invitational Exhibition,
American Academy of Arts and
Letters, NY.
Friends of Daniel Robbins,
Museum of Art, Rhode Island
School of Design, Providence.
1995-1996
*Three Sculptors and Their
Drawings*, Grounds for
Sculpture, Hamilton, NJ.
1994-1999
Outdoor Sculpture Center,
Kouros Gallery, Ridgefield, CT.
1993
Hands On, Washington Art
Association, Washington, CT.
1992
*Sculpture Fields at Sagaponic
Close*, Southampton, NY.
Largescale, Bill Bace Gallery, NY.
1991
Proposals, Nina Owen Gallery,
Chicago, IL.
Artists at Home: Furniture,
Bill Bace Gallery, NY.
1990
The Significant Surface,
Philadelphia Art Alliance, PA.
1988
Courtyard Sculpture, Hudson
River Museum, Yonkers, NY.
1987
New Works by Old Friends,
De Cordova Museum and
Sculpture Park, Lincoln, MA.
1986
50th Year Anniversary,
Sculptors Guild, NY.
Yankee Bronze Casting, The
William Benton Museum of Art,
University of Connecticut, Storrs.
1985
*Between Abstraction and
Reality*, Marilyn Pearl Gallery,
NY.

1984
Invitational Exhibition, National
Academy of Design, NY.
The Ways of Wood, O.I.A.
(Organization of Independent
Artists), NY.
1983
*Aspects of Abstraction: Three
Sculptors*, Colby College
Museum of Art, Waterville, ME.
1982
Four Artists and a Writer,
Federal Hall, NY.
1980
*Arte Contemporanea
Americana*, Palazzo Venezia,
Rome, Italy.
*O.I.A. Outdoor Sculpture
Exhibition*, Wards Island, NY.
Invitational Exhibition, Greater
Hartford Arts Council, CT.
1979
*Allegoria dell'Inpronte
Digitale, Italian and American
Drawings*, Galleria Il Mercato
del Sale, Milan, Italy.
1978
Operation Rebuild, Museum of
Contemporary Art, Udine, Italy
(traveled).
1976
Works on Paper, Marilyn Pearl
Gallery, NY.
1974
Sculpture in the Park, De
Cordova Museum and
Sculpture Park, Lincoln, MA.
1972
Acquistions, Weatherspoon Art
Gallery, University of North
Carolina at Greensboro.
1971
Art New York, Zabriskie
Gallery, NY.
1970
Sculpture in the Spring, The

William Benton Museum of
Art, University of Connecticut,
Storrs.
New Acquisitions, University
Gallery, University of
Massachusetts at Amherst.
1969
Drawings, The Baltimore
Museum of Art, MD.

Selected Commissions and Public Collections

The William Benton Museum
  of Art, University of
  Connecticut, Storrs.
Jack S. Blanton Museum of
  Art, University of Texas at
  Austin.
Brooklyn Museum of Art, NY.
Cape Ann Historical Museum,
  Gloucester, MA.
The Corcoran Gallery of Art,
  Washington, DC.
De Cordova Museum and
  Sculpture Park, Lincoln, MA.
Elrod Sculpture Garden, Palm
  Springs Desert Museum, CA.
Marsh Art Gallery, University
  of Richmond Museums, VA.
Museum of Art, Rhode Island
  School of Design,
  Providence, RI.
Museum of Art and Archeology,
  University of Missouri,
  Columbia.
Museum of Contemporary Art,
  Udine, Italy.
Trent University, Ontario,
  Canada (outdoor sculpture).
University Gallery, University
  of Massachusetts at Amherst.
Villa San Lorenzo, Assisi, Italy
  (fountain).
Weatherspoon Art Gallery,
  University of North Carolina
  at Greensboro.

Dimensions are given in inches, height precedes width precedes depth. Works are lent courtesy of the artist unless otherwise indicated. Catalogue numbers with asterisks indicate works that are included in the exhibition at the Muscarelle Museum of Art, The College of William and Mary.

1. **Quarry Piece #3**
    1976, welded steel, 54 x 22 x 16

2. **Maquette for Pylon**
    1991, wood, stains, 5 x 6 x 9
    Marsh Art Gallery, University of Richmond Museums, Gift of the artist

3. **Pylon**
    1991, welded steel, polychromed,
    37 x 31 x 40
    Marsh Art Gallery, University of Richmond Museums, Gift of Bernard and Ninon Chaet
    (illustrated, page 35)

4.* **Maquette for Omphalos**
    1991, welded steel, 6 x 6 x 6

5.* **Omphalos**
    1991-92, welded steel, 79 x 72 x 122
    (illustrated, page 37)

6.* **Shield of Dirac**
    1991-92, steel, polychromed, 30 x 30 x 5

7.* **Field**
    1993, wood, polychromed, 43 x 68 x 13

8.* **Tower**
    1993-94, wood, polychromed, 86 x 33 x 50

9.* **Sanctus**
    1994, wood, polychromed, 58 x 35 x 35
    Collection of Anthea Fane
    (illustrated, page 39)

10.* **Mound**
    1994, wood, polychromed, 17 x 13 x 16
    (illustrated, page 41)

11. **Column**
    1994, wood and steel, 49 x 14 x 8

12.* **Center 1**
    1994, wood, 21 x 52 x 56
    Collection of Dimitri Fane
    (illustrated, page 43)

13.* **Chamber**
    1996, wood, polychromed, 32 x 12 x 28
    Lent courtesy of Kouros Gallery, New York
    (illustrated, page 45)

14.* **Monument**
    1996, wood (poplar), 68 x 50 x 24
    Lent courtesy of Kouros Gallery, New York

15. **Mantle**
1996-97, wood, 25 x 38 x 28
Lent courtesy of Kouros Gallery, New York
(illustrated, page 47)

16.* **Drain**
1996, wood and steel, 35 x 7 x 6
Lent courtesy of Kouros Gallery, New York

17.* **Taccola's Dream**
1997, wood, 41 x 84 x 31
Lent courtesy of Kouros Gallery, New York
(illustrated, page 49)

18.* **Duct**
1997, wood, polychromed, 28 x 23 x 11
Lent courtesy of Kouros Gallery, New York

19. **Barrel**
1997-98, wood and steel, 27 x 24 x 8
Lent courtesy of Kouros Gallery, New York
(illustrated, page 51)

20.* **Pendant**
1998, wood and steel, 27 x 8 x 11
Lent courtesy of Kouros Gallery, New York
(illustrated, page 53)

21.* **Mill Piece**
1998, wood, polychromed, 73 x 42 x 60
Lent courtesy of Kouros Gallery, New York
(illustrated, page 55)

22. **Cask**
1999, concrete and wood, 46 x 18 x 28
(illustrated, page 57)

23. **Table**
1999-2000, wood, stains, 39 x 9 x 36
(illustrated, page 59)

24. **Roller**
1999-2000, wood, 33 x 18 x 39
(illustrated, page 61)

25. **Source**
2000, concrete and wood, 54 x 22 x 26
(illustrated, page 63)

26. **Conduit**
2000, concrete and wood, stains,
62 x 47 x 86
(illustrated, page 6; detail, cover)

27. **Colmar**
2000, wood, cement, plastic, stains,
59 x 30 x 18
(illustrated, frontispiece)

28.* **Mount**
2001, concrete, stains, 15 x 12 x 17
(illustrated, page 65)

29. **Filter**
2001, concrete and steel, stains,
20 x 17 x 10
(illustrated, page 67)

30. **Marsh Conduit**
2001, concrete and wood (white oak),
aluminum, copper, stains, 67 x 37 x 53